garden mosaics
MADE EASY

garden mosaics
MADE EASY

CLIFF KENNEDY AND JANE WENDLING POMPILIO

North Light Books
Cincinnati, Ohio

www.artistsnetwork.com

Garden Mosaics Made Easy. Copyright © 2006 by Cliff Kennedy and Jane Wendling Pompilio. Manufactured in China. All rights reserved. The patterns and drawings in the book are for personal use of reader. By permission of the author and publisher, they may be either hand-traced or photocopied to make single copies, but under no circumstances may they be resold or republished. It is permissible for the purchaser to make the projects contained herein and sell them at fairs, bazaars and craft shows. No other part of this book may be reproduced in any form or by any electronic or mechanical means including information storage and retrieval systems without permission in writing from the publisher, except by a reviewer, who may quote a brief passage in review. Published by North Light Books, an imprint of F+W Publications, Inc., 4700 East Galbraith Road, Cincinnati, Ohio 45236. (800) 289-0963. First edition.

10 09 08 07 06   5 4 3 2 1

Distributed in Canada by Fraser Direct
100 Armstrong Avenue
Georgetown, ON, Canada L7G 5S4
Tel: (905) 877-4411

Distributed in the U.K. and Europe by David & Charles
Brunel House, Newton Abbot, Devon, TQ12 4PU, England
Tel: (+44) 1626 323200, Fax: (+44) 1626 323319
Email: mail@davidandcharles.co.uk

Distributed in Australia by Capricorn Link
P.O. Box 704, S. Windsor, NSW 2756 Australia
Tel: (02) 4577-3555

Library of Congress Cataloging-in-Publication Data
Kennedy, Cliff
    Garden mosaics made easy / Cliff Kennedy and Jane Wendling Pompilio.
        p. cm.
    Includes index.
    ISBN-13: 978-158180-720-2
    ISBN-10: 1-58180-720-1 (alk. paper)
    1. Garden ornaments and furniture. 2. Mosaics. I. Pompilio, Jane Wendling, II. Title.
    SB473.5k45 2006
    717--dc22
                                        2005015168

fw
F+W PUBLICATIONS, INC.

Editor: David Oeters
Cover Designer: Karla Baker
Designers: Leigh Ann Lentz and Marissa Bowers
Layout Artist: Jessica Schultz
Production Coordinator: Jennifer Wagner
Photographers: Tim Grondin, Christine Polomsky and Jane Pompilio
Photo Stylist: Nora Martini

METRIC CONVERSION CHART

TO CONVERT	TO	MULTIPLY BY
Inches	Centimeters	2.54
Centimeters	Inches	0.4
Feet	Centimeters	30.5
Centimeters	Feet	0.03
Yards	Meters	0.9
Meters	Yards	1.1
Sq. Inches	Sq. Centimeters	6.45
Sq. Centimeters	Sq. Inches	0.16
Sq. Feet	Sq. Meters	0.09
Sq. Meters	Sq. Feet	10.8
Sq. Yards	Sq. Meters	0.8
Sq. Meters	Sq. Yards	1.2
Pounds	Kilograms	0.45
Kilograms	Pounds	2.2
Ounces	Grams	28.4
Grams	Ounces	0.04

DEDICATION

To our families and friends who have supported and encouraged us throughout our lives and made life worth living.

ABOUT THE AUTHORS

Jane Wendling Pompilio, a former elementary school teacher, is a mom to Lauren and two Jasons (one a son-in-law). Always with pencil in hand and eager to create, Jane has found Kaleidoscope Stained Glass in the MainStrasse Village of Covington, Kentucky, to be a haven for developing and creating new stained glass and mosaic designs. Teaching art classes and spending time with new friends from all walks of life and from all over the world have made her experience at Kaleidoscope a special treasure.

Cliff Kennedy owns and operates Kaleidoscope Stained Glass. After perfecting his art glass hobby, Cliff opened his studio doors for retail sales, commissioned work, restoration, repair and hands-on instructional classes. He has also taught classes at Northern Kentucky University. Proud to be a Marine and the father of three sons, Cliff enjoys his creative profession during the week and writing on the weekend.

Jane and Cliff are authors of the book *Creative Techniques for Stained Glass*, also by North Light Books.

ACKNOWLEDGMENTS

A special thank-you to Howard and Gloria Wendling, who have helped us in many ways at Kaleidoscope and provided the beautiful location for many of the photos in this book.

Thank you to Molly Merten, whose wonderful graphic design talents and sincere interest have made our previous books beautiful. Thanks to Carly Emmerich, whose graphic arts skills helped us perfect our drawings, and to all our friends at Wendling Printing who helped us get started in the book business.

Thank you to our awesome editor, David Oeters, who brought knowledge and talent to this endeavor and tirelessly encouraged us throughout this adventure.

Our thanks to Christine Polomsky and Tim Grondin, our photographers extraordinaire, who motivated us throughout this book and gave us terrific results. Thanks also to Leigh Ann Lentz and her beautiful design work, and Nora Martini for her talents as a stylist.

Finally, thank you to Tricia Waddell and Christine Doyle, who believed in us, and to Liz Nash, who brought us on this journey. We thank you all for another great experience with wonderful people!

Contents

Introduction   9

Materials   10
Tools   12
Basic Techniques   14
- Breaking glass and china   14
- Cutting glass   15
- Using the direct method   16
- Using the indirect method   17
- Using grout and sealant   18
- Solving problems   19

Garden Mosaic Projects   20
- Preening Mirror   22
- Flower Box Posies   26
- Glass Tile House Number   30
- Flower Petal Ceiling Light   34
- Butterfly Feeder Stone   38
- Birdbath Saucer   42
- Birdbath Base   46
- Garden Chime   50
- Butterfly Tile   54
- Catch a Falling Star   58
- Seaside Garden Brick   62
- Garden Thermometer   66
- Country Clock   70
- Sailor's Delight   74
- Stained Glass Flower   78
- Garden Tabletop   82
- Blooming Daisies Garden Stone   86
- Fish Fountain   90
- Landscape Photo   94
- Tulips Garden Stone   98
- Bunny Plaque   102
- Summer Poppies   106
- Seaside Village Garden Stone   110
- Coneflower Garden Stone   114
- Lily and Dragonfly Garden Stone   118

Gallery   122
Resources   126
Index   127

For Cliff and I, some of our finest memories revolve around the garden. One of my earliest garden memories is of the brightly colored chrysanthemums my dad planted along the border of our family garden. Cliff vividly recalls his grandmother working the soil around her house with an old hoe, then planting flowers in the fertile ground. With time and patience, the seeds sprouted and grew into the fullest, most colorful, plate-sized blooms one could imagine.

It's no wonder the wonderful memories of the garden have become the inspiration for the mosaics in this book. Like a garden, these mosaics are filled with beauty, joy, surprise and color. The lively yellow, vibrant orange and white of the chrysanthemums have found a place in my memory, and in the colors, textures and the seemingly random mix of glass, tiles and china that make each mosaic such a beautiful work of art.

In these projects, you'll find a butterfly fluttering on a mosaic tile, a coneflower on a stepping-stone, a field of poppies in a gorgeous frame and a wind chime that speaks softly when the wind blows. There is a wealth of inspiration for mosaics waiting in every garden.

Bring the beauty of mosaics to your garden and home. Place a gorgeous mosaic star, made of rich orange, yellow and streaky pink glass, beside your favorite flowers, letting the colors come to life in your garden. A garden mosaic in a picture frame will make a welcome addition to any room or window, while beautiful blue glass tiles make a striking flower petal ceiling light. Store your mosaics inside during the winter, offering a welcome reminder of the joy of spring.

We hope the projects in this book will inspire you to enjoy the beauty in nature, and remind you of the garden memories that are waiting to be shared.

Jane Wending Pompili

Materials

In every mosaic you can find three basic types of material: the surface that holds the mosaic; the tesserae, which are the small pieces used to create a mosaic; and finally, the adhesive and sealant which secures and protects the tesserae on the surface. You can make your mosaics as simple or complex as you like, depending on the materials you choose. Be creative and inspired as you work, and look for materials that are exciting and beautiful.

Surfaces

Almost any solid surface has the potential to become part of a mosaic, but choosing the right surface for your project is often the key to success.

Choose a surface that will support the tesserae and adhesive and work with your design. Pre-formed stepping-stones and bricks make excellent surfaces for your mosaics, and look beautiful. Garden stone molds allow you to create your own surfaces with a concrete mix. The smooth surface of tiles are stylish and fun to decorate. Try terra-cotta products, with preparation they make excellent surfaces for mosaics.

Hobby, craft, stained glass stores and garden centers carry table bases and other display products that are suitable mosaic surfaces. Landscape stores and nurseries carry specialty stones and marble pieces that can be decorated. Search yard sales and flea markets for treasures waiting to become part of a mosaic. Simple wood and glass surfaces can also become a tabletop or decorative mosaic.

Tesserae

A small piece of glass, marble or tile used in a mosaic was once known as tessera, but today the term can be applied to anything that you use in a mosaic design.

Glass: With so many types of glass available, a clever crafter has a wealth of options for mosaic tesserae. Craft stores carry a wide selection of packaged glass designed to be used in mosaics.

Stained glass stores have a wonderful selection of specialty colored glass and glass-cutting supplies, as well as faceted jewels, nuggets, scrap glass and shaped glass pieces. You'll also find specialty mirror glass and beautiful iridized tiles. It's well worth a trip to a local store to see the colors and be inspired. Look for other glass tesserae and found glass pieces, such as beach glass, which is frosted and has worn, smooth edges.

Tile: A tile store or home improvement center is the perfect place to search for tiles of all shapes, sizes and colors. Flat stones glued to a mesh background, which can be found in tile stores, offer a more natural-looking tile tesserae.

China: Flea markets and yard sales are great places to find chipped plates, decorative dishes or pieces of china. Household "accidents" are another great source for china tesserae.

Other materials: Rocks, shells and mementos, such as ceramic figurines, can be incorporated into mosaics. Look around for other possible tesserae, just be aware of the effects of weathering and aging on the tesserae you choose, and know what adhesives will be necessary to secure it. Polymer clay, metal, toys, plastic decorations and more could find its way into your projects.

TESSERAE clockwise starting at top left: shells, glass nuggets, china, glass tiles, rocks, ceramic tiles and glass.

■■ ■ ■ ■ **TIP** ■ ■ ■ ■ ■

Silver-colored tape, available at stained glass stores, can be added to the back of translucent cathedral glass to make the color more vivid and reflective in the sunshine.

ADHESIVE AND SEALANTS clockwise starting at top left: *craft glue, sealant, concrete mix, terra-cotta grout, white grout, cement-based adhesive and silicone.*

Adhesives and Sealants

An adhesive secures tesserae on a surface. With so many types of tesserae and surfaces, it's important to choose the right adhesive. A good sealant will help make your mosaic a lasting treasure.

Mosaic adhesive: Visit your local craft or hardware store to find adhesives for your mosaic. Read the labels carefully to find one that best suits your project and will bond to both the tesserae and the surface. Craft and school glue works well on porous surfaces and is safe for young crafters. A cement-based adhesive, such as the Liquid Nails Clear Adhesive used in this book, works best with glass and tile pieces. It is an effective adhesive for outdoor projects. We also used silicone, which is more flexible than other adhesives. E6000 is a rubber-based compound that offers exceptionally strong adhesive properties. Weldbond is another good adhesive for indoor projects. It creates a strong bond that dries clear and doesn't give off fumes.

Concrete mix: A concrete mix can be used to secure tesserae, especially in mosaics made using the indirect method (see page 17 for information on the indirect method). Read the instructions carefully when using a concrete mix. The concrete should dry overnight or longer, depending on the humidity and weather conditions. Be aware that concrete may not set fully for 28 days. We prefer a sand mix because it provides a reasonably smooth surface, as well as strength for

outdoor projects. Specialty concrete mixes dry in less than an hour and come in a variety of colors.

Grout: Grout is a mix that fills the space between the tesserae, and protects and supports tesserae after they've been secured to the surface. It comes in many colors and styles. Latex is included in many types of grout to provide strength and durability for outdoor use. You can purchase grout at a local craft store, or from a home improvement center. Follow the package instructions for application. Bags of grout may differ slightly in color. If you'll need more than one bag of grout to complete a project, combine the bags to keep the color consistent.

Sealant: Some surfaces need to be sealed before you begin a project. Seal terra cotta with a mix of half wood or craft glue and half water. Seal outdoor wood surfaces with marine varnish. When you finish an outdoor project, you may want to cover it with a grout sealant. It will protect your work from moisture and aging. Apply grout sealant only after the grout and concrete have set fully. You'll find grout sealant in the tile section of your local home improvement center.

Tools

You don't need many tools to start creating beautiful mosaics, and most can be found around the house. Refer to the material lists before each project for a more complete list of the tools. For specialty tools, such as those used in glass cutting, check out stained glass stores, home improvement centers and your local hobby and craft stores.

 ## Basic Tools

Below are some simple tools that you'll use for many of the projects in this book. It's a good idea to collect these tools beforehand and have them ready for your mosaic projects.

Scissors or mosaic pattern shears: Many of the projects in this book use a pattern. Once you transfer it from the book, you'll need scissors to cut out the pattern. Mosaic pattern shears are a specialty tool that allows you to cut out a pattern and leave space for grout between the tesserae.

Carbon paper, pencil and permanent marker: You can use carbon paper and a pencil to transfer the pattern to your mosaic surface. You can also draw the pattern on the surface freehand. If the pattern is hard to discern, use a permanent marker to trace over the lines.

Adhesive paper: Adhesive paper will help protect delicate surface areas when grouting. It's also useful for transferring the mosaic in the indirect method.

Hammer: You'll need a hammer for breaking glass, tile and china pieces for your mosaic projects. See page 14 for more information on breaking glass safely. A hammer can also be used to settle concrete in a mold.

Old towels: Old towels are useful for breaking glass or china and for cleaning your mosaics.

Molds: Create your own stepping stones, or create direct or indirect mosaics in concrete, using a mold. You can find molds of various sizes and shapes in hobby and craft stores, stained glass shops, landscape stores and nurseries.

Latex gloves: Concrete and grout can dry out bare skin. Protect your hands with a good pair of latex gloves.

Protective goggles: Wear protective goggles when mixing concrete or grout, or grinding glass.

Putty knife or brass wire brush: Clean your mosaic after the grout and concrete have dried with these useful tools.

BASIC TOOLS clockwise starting at top left: *brass wire brush, putty knife, protective goggles, adhesive paper, scissors, old towel, latex gloves, carbon paper and pencils, molds and hammer.*

Glass-Cutting Tools

Although all of the projects can be done using broken glass pieces, some of the patterns are designed for shaped and cut glass pieces, which require special tools to finish. Look on page 15 for more information on glass-cutting techniques.

Glass cutter: We've found that a pistol-grip glass cutter is the easiest way to cut glass. A self-oiling cutting wheel and an easy-to-hold handle make it simple to cut pieces of glass using a pattern. The cutter scores the glass for easy, controlled breakage.

Running pliers: These pliers have a set of curved and padded jaws with a central guide mark on the top jaw. They aid in breaking glass along score lines.

Grozing pliers: These pliers assist in breaking glass, especially small or curved pieces that are more difficult to break. They have spring-tension handles and curved, serrated jaws for gripping glass.

Electric glass grinder: The diamond-coated grinding head of an electric glass grinder rotates against the edge of a glass piece, smoothing out the jagged spots to better fit the pattern. Always wear protective eyewear, and remove any jewelry when using the grinder.

Glass and tile nippers: These pliers are specifically made for breaking pieces of glass and tile into a desired shape. The cutting blades break the glass and tile in a quick, easy pinching motion.

GLASS-CUTTING TOOLS clockwise starting at top left: *Electric glass grinder, pistol-grip glass cutter, running pliers, glass and tile nippers, and grozing pliers.*

TIP

When using the electric glass grinder, always keep the water reservoir inside the machine filled so the sponge and grinding wheel stay wet; never grind glass on a dry wheel.

Basic Techniques

Creating a mosaic is simple. You don't need complicated tools or years of practice to create a beautiful mosaic that you'll be proud to display. With just a few basic techniques, you'll be making mosaics in no time at all!

In this section, you'll learn how to break glass and china, and cut glass to make shaped tesserae. You'll discover two easy methods for creating a mosaic, and learn how to apply grout and sealant to a mosaic to protect it. Finally, you'll find a few basic problem-solving tips to take the worry out of your work.

Breaking glass and china

Breaking glass and china for mosaic pieces is a fun, simple way to create tesserae, but it can be dangerous. There are a few steps you can take to break glass or china safely and efficiently. You don't want the glass or china to shatter into pieces that are too small to use, and you want the broken pieces to be well contained.

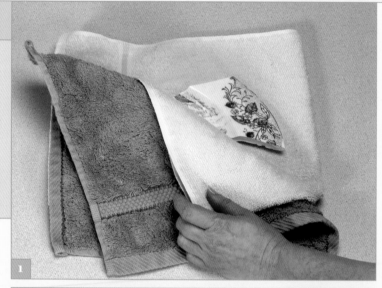

1 Prepare glass
Always wear protective goggles when breaking glass. Place the china or glass between several layers of old towels, making sure it is well contained and gathered in the center of the towels.

2 Break glass
Use a hammer on the towels to break the china or glass. Use enough force to crack and break the pieces, but not so much that it shatters.

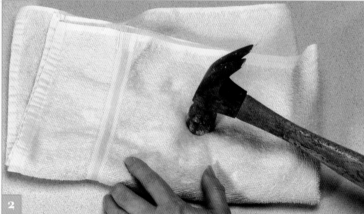

3 Check glass
Open the towels to check the broken glass or china. If you desire smaller pieces, close the towel and use the hammer again.

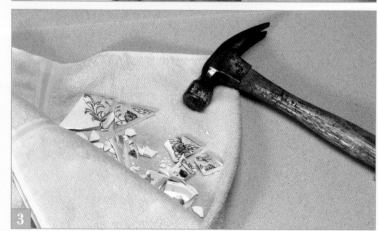

TIP

A rubber mallet can be used instead of a hammer to break china and glass for mosaics. You'll still need to wrap the tesserae in a towel before you use the mallet.

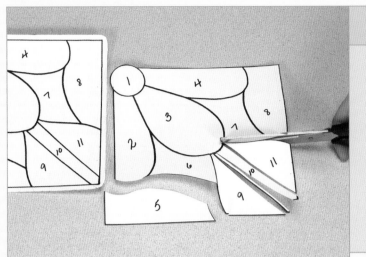

Cutting glass

You may want to use shaped glass pieces for some of the projects in this book. Cutting glass is much easier than you might think. A glass cutter doesn't actually "cut" glass but makes a score line that allows for a clean, controlled break. It's a good idea to practice making score lines on scrap glass until you feel comfortable holding the cutter and scoring the glass.

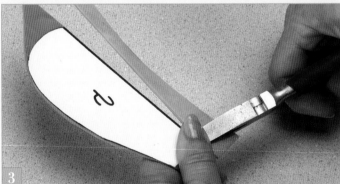

1 Cut pattern

Make two copies of the pattern. Number the pattern pieces, making sure the copies match. Cut out the pattern pieces from one pattern using mosaic shears or scissors. If you use scissors, make extra thick lines with a marker, and cut on either side of the line. This will allow space for the grout between the mosaic pieces.

2 Score glass

Use spray adhesive to attach the pattern pieces to the appropriately colored glass. Use a glass cutter to score the glass along the edge of the pattern lines. Never run the glass cutter more than once over a score line.

3 Break glass

Use grozing pliers to break off the small or curved pieces of glass, and running pliers to break the straight lines in the glass.

4 Grind glass

Lay the numbered pieces of glass over the duplicate pattern, making sure the numbers match. If the glass doesn't fit the pattern, use the electric glass grinder to trim the pieces. Lay the glass on the grid surface of the grinding machine. Turn on the machine, and then, slowly and with a single motion, run the edge of the glass along the griding wheel. Grind until the edges are smooth and match the edge of the affixed pattern. Note: Always wear protective goggles when using a glass grinder.

Using the direct method

After you gather your tesserae, the next step is to assemble the mosaic. There are two methods of constructing a mosaic: the direct and the indirect. In the direct method, tesserae is placed directly on the mosaic surface. They can be placed in drying concrete, or glued on a prepared surface, as we have done in this example. This method allows you to easily make adjustments to the mosaic as you work.

1 Prepare surface
Make sure your surface is clean. If you're using a pattern, transfer the pattern onto the surface using carbon paper and a pencil, or by drawing it freehand.

2 Begin mosaic
Begin laying your tesserae on the surface, following the pattern lines. Once you're satisfied with a section, use an adhesive to secure the tesserae in place.

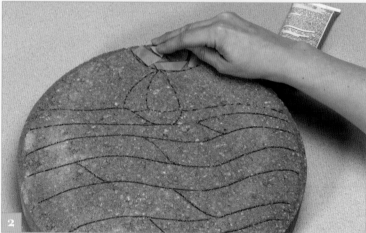

3 Finish mosaic
Continue laying the tesserae directly on the surface, securing them in place with the adhesive. When complete, check to make sure all the tesserae are secured by the adhesive. Use a craft knife to clean any adhesive that has oozed from the tessera edges and dried. If desired, grout the mosaic to help secure the tesserae to the surface. See page 18 for more information on using grout.

 TIP

Goo Gone or acetone nail polish remover are excellent products for cleaning mosaics. Both are effective at removing adhesive residue from the top of tesserae.

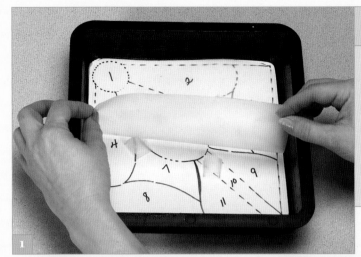

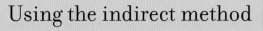

Using the indirect method

In the indirect method of creating a mosaic, an adhesive sheet is placed over a pattern, then tesserae are applied to the sheet. The assembled tesserae is placed on the mosaic surface, or concrete is poured over the tesserae, as we have done in this example. This method creates mosaics with a smooth, even surface.

1 Prepare mold

Prepare the mold by liberally smearing petroleum jelly on the sides. Using a light box or a sunny window, trace the pattern on the back of the paper so that it appears in reverse. Lay the pattern facedown in the mold. Place an adhesive sheet on the pattern and trim to fit. Remove the backing of the adhesive sheet and lay it, sticky side up, on the pattern. Use tape to secure the adhesive sheet to the pattern.

2 Begin mosaic

If you are using cut-glass pieces in the mosaic, make sure you transfer the numbers to the back side of the pattern. Following the pattern, which should appear reverse in the mold, lay tesserae on the adhesive sheet. Lay the tesserae facedown, so the back of each piece faces you. Position the tesserae to keep the spacing between pieces as even as possible.

3 Add concrete

Prepare the concrete and pour it over the pattern in the mold, stopping just below the top of the mold. Tap the edges of the mold with a hammer to release bubbles and settle the concrete mix. Let it dry overnight. Check the concrete package, however, as drying times may vary.

4 Remove mold

When dry, carefully pry the mosaic from the mold. Remove the adhesive paper, then use a rag, putty knife or brass wire brush to clean the mosaic. Concrete is not completely cured for about 28 days. Allow the mosaic to cure before setting it outside.

Using grout and sealant

After you finish laying your tesserae, you can help secure the mosaic with grout and a sealant. Grout comes in many different colors and two different forms: sanded and unsanded. Sanded is denser and can be used to fill almost any size space between mosaic pieces. Unsanded grout is usually less coarse and should be used for grout lines no wider than ⅛" (3mm). Sealant helps protect your mosaic from water, dirt, weathering and discoloration. While not all mosaic projects need to be grouted or sealed, using grout can highlight the mosaic and help secure the tesserae to the surface.

1 Mix grout
Prepare the grout following the instructions on the package. The grout should be the consistency of cake batter. Add water slowly and mix thoroughly until you are satisfied with the consistency.

2 Pour grout
Pour the grout directly over the center of the mosaic.

3 Spread grout
Spread the grout over the entire mosaic, making sure to fill in the cracks between the mosaic pieces. Let the grout dry for about 10 minutes before continuing.

4 Clean mosiac
Use a rag and putty knife to clean the project, scraping away the grout on the mosaic pieces. Brush the excess from the edges. Make sure you don't scrape grout from between the mosaic pieces. If necessary, repair any gaps with leftover grout.

5 Apply sealant
Store the mosaic in a safe place to let the grout completely dry. Depending on the conditions where you keep the mosaic and the grout you use, it may take a month for the grout to completely dry. Consult the instructions that came with the grout for exact drying times. Once the grout is dry, apply sealant to the mosaic to protect it from the outdoor elements and weathering. Test your sealant first to make sure it doesn't discolor the grout. Using sealant with moisture still trapped in the grout may cause discoloration and cracking.

■ ■ ■ ■ ■ TIP ■ ■ ■ ■ ■
Never dry grout in direct sunlight or use heat to speed drying time. This will cause the grout to cure too fast and crack.

Solving problems

One of the most enjoyable aspects of creating mosaics is how easy it is to master and create beautiful art. Beautiful tesserae are easy to find, inspiration is everywhere and there are few problems that can't be solved with a little ingenuity. Below we've collected some quick fixes for your projects.

Pattern transfer

If the pattern doesn't transfer well using carbon paper, go over the lines with a permanent black marker. Or, cut out the pattern pieces and trace the shapes onto the surface.

Cleaning glue from mosaic

If glue fills the cracks between tesserae, the grout won't secure the mosaic to the surface. Use a pencil or toothpick to clean out the still-moist glue, giving the grout room to seal the space between tesserae.

Air bubbles

If the mosaic comes out of the mold with air bubbles (little spots on the surface of the concrete), spread grout that matches the concrete over the air bubbles for a quick fix.

Loose tesserae

If you have tessearae that are still loose even after the grout and concrete have dried, add grout to the edges of the loose pieces until they are attached firmly. Scrape the grout into the gaps, making sure to keep the surface smooth. Once the grout has dried, the pieces should be attached firmly.

PERIWINKLE

garden mosaic
projects

Nothing can compare to the beauty found during a stroll through the garden. The heady and relaxing scent of gorgeous flowers fills the air. Warm rays of sunshine caress your face. Flowers grow like clouds of color over the ground and butterflies flutter from bloom to bloom. The mosaics in this book will help you bring that beauty into your home or garden.

You'll find a wealth of beautiful mosaic designs in this book. There's a delightful wind chime made from a terra-cotta pot, as well as a birdbath saucer and base decorated with gorgeous iridescent mosaic tile. A butterfly, inspired by a piece of fabric, flutters on a tile, while a garden stepping-stone is decorated with a star for your very own garden walk of fame! In one project, tulips climb up a rectangular stepping-stone; another features a flower inspired by a stained glass window. A child's drawing finds immortality in a stained glass mosaic stepping-stone. You'll be amazed at the objects you can decorate with mosaics, from clocks to thermometers, bricks to tiles, and ceiling lights, flower boxes and tabletops.

Whether you decorate your yard, porch or patio, bring a bit of the garden into your home or give a mosaic gift that a friend or loved one will cherish forever. May these projects add color and beauty to your life!

preening mirror

Give the birds in your garden a place to gather and admire their reflection with this mirror. Place this mirror among your flower beds to reflect all the hard work you've done. Your feathered guests will be delighted by this simple project.

This project uses tiles, nuggets and a mirror, and it can be finished in no time at all! Change the border motif and use a larger tile, or use a sheet of wood as a base. With so many possibilities, this project has plenty of opportunities to make it uniquely your own.

MATERIALS AND TOOLS

- 8" x 8" (20cm x 20cm) ceramic tile
- 1" x 1" (3cm x 3cm) teal ceramic tiles
- Glass nuggets
- 5½" (14cm) square mirror
- Clear cement-based adhesive
- Adhesive paper
- Scissors

- Paint scraper
- Latex gloves
- Container
- Mixing tool
- Old towel
- White grout
- Sealant

1 Place tiles

Place the 1" (3cm) teal tiles evenly around the perimeter of the 8" (20cm) square tile, making sure to leave space for the glass nuggets. Check the placement of the teal tiles by placing the mirror and the glass nuggets on the square tile. When you are satisfied with the placement, remove the mirror and glass nuggets and secure the the teal tiles with the adhesive. Note: Tiles are often sold on mesh. If tile on mesh is available, don't remove the tile from the mesh. Cut strips of the tile and mesh and arrange the strips around the border. You'll find this is much easier to work with than individual tiles.

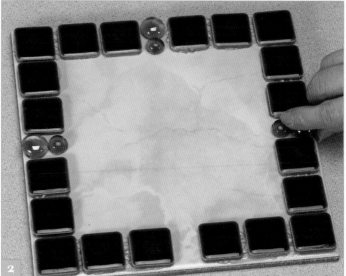

2 Place glass nuggets

Adhere the glass nuggets between the tiles.

3 Place mirror

Adhere the mirror to the tile, centered inside the teal tile border.

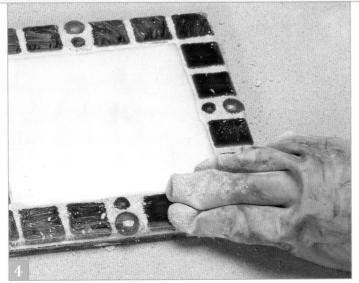

4 Grout and seal

Cover the mirror with adhesive paper, making sure there are no gaps at the edges. Put on latex gloves, then grout the tile border. See page 18 for more information on grouting.

5 Finish mirror

After letting the grout dry for 10 minutes, carefully pull up the adhesive paper. Make sure you're not removing the grout between the tiles. Clean the grout from the tile with an old towel. Repair any imperfections with leftover grout. Once the grout is completely dry, apply sealant to the tile and grout. When finished, clean grout or sealant from the mirror with a paint scraper and an old towel.

Take Another Look

Try to match the color of the tile with the colors in your garden. This project is a beautiful addition to a flower bed. Tinker with the placement of the tesserae and try different colors of tile or grout, or experiment with different glass nuggets or other tesserae before adhering them to the tile. Keep trying different variations until you're satisfied with the results.

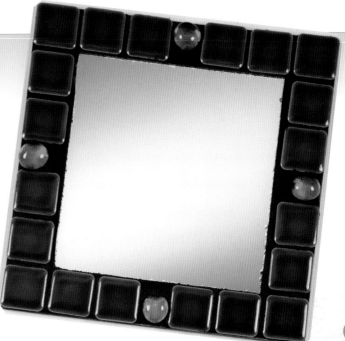

flower box posies

Turn a plain planter box into a work of whimsical art by adding pressed-glass flowers and iridized squares that add sparkle to your project.

This project is designed to be groutless, but there's no reason you couldn't add grout to help secure the mosaic. This idea can be transferred easily to any container shape. Just make sure that when you choose an adhesive, you read the package carefully to be certain that it will secure the tesserae on the surface.

MATERIALS AND TOOLS

- Purchased planter box, 10" x 5" x 6" deep (25cm x 13cm x 15cm)
- Precut pressed-glass flower shapes (Diamond Tech International)
- 3/8" (10mm) glass squares in iridized blue, iridized green and opaque green
- Clear cement-based adhesive
- Wood glue
- Water
- Pattern PAGE 29

- Paintbrush
- Small bowl
- Carbon paper and pencil
- Razor blade

1 Prepare flower box

Seal the flower box by creating a mixture of equal parts wood glue and water, then use a paintbrush to cover the whole flower box with the mixture. Let dry.

2 Transfer pattern

Use carbon paper to transfer the pattern on page 29 to the front of the flower box. Lay the carbon paper on the front of the box, then lay the pattern on the carbon paper. Carefully use a pencil to trace firmly over the lines on the pattern. You may want to draw the pattern on the box freehand instead of using carbon paper and pencil.

3 Place flowers

Adhere the pressed-glass flowers first, then adhere iridized green glass squares along the lines to form the stems below the flowers. Because you won't be sealing the project with grout, make sure you use adhesive sparingly so it doesn't ooze, but does secure the tesserae.

 TIP

Weather conditions can affect your projects. Read the instructions on your adhesive very carefully. Some projects may need to be moved indoors during severe weather.

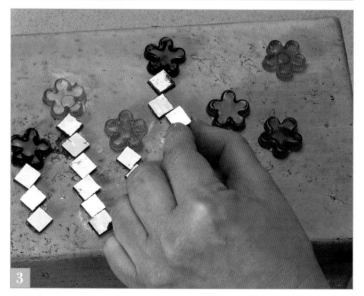

4 Place grass and sky

Apply glass squares for the grass and the sky. Use iridized blue squares for the sky and opaque green for the grass. Use the adhesive sparingly, but make sure the mosaic pieces are secure.

5 Clean mosaic

When finished, clean the squares using a razor blade to remove the excess dried adhesive from the mosaic pieces.

■ ■ ■ enlarge the flower box posies pattern to 147% ■ ■ ■

glass tile
house number

Make a house your home with this glass tile house number. Place the mosaic in a flower bed in front of your house or in the middle of a garden, or place it on the front porch surrounded by potted plants or flowers for a cozy invitation for your guests.

There are so many beautiful tiles on the market. Some are made of glass and others made of ceramic; some are a single color and others streaky and iridized. Spend some time browsing your local craft or tile store, or a home improvement center, for the perfect tile. Whatever you choose, this project is sure to be a winner!

MATERIALS AND TOOLS

- 12" x 12" (30cm x 30cm) concrete stepping stone
- 1" (3cm) glass tiles (purchased or cut) in iridized cobalt blue, sky blue and turquoise
- Clear cement-based adhesive
- Masking tape
- Ruler
- Pencil
- Permanent black marker (optional)
- Latex gloves

- Container
- Mixing tool
- Old towel
- Black grout
- Sealant

Note: When planning colors for this project, try to use a dark color for the number and a more muted color for the background. This will help the number stand out.

1 Create pattern

Create a grid pattern on the stepping stone. Make 1" (3cm) marks along each side of the stepping stone, then use a ruler to make straight lines horizontally and vertically across the stone. You should have a grid of 1" (3cm) squares over the stone when finished. Use a pencil to make the marks at first. Use a permanent marker for darker lines. Find the center of the stone by making a line from the center of each side across the grid. The center is where the lines meet.

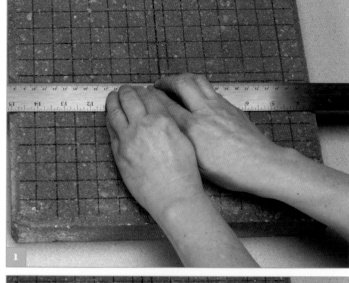

2 Plan numbers

Using the grid on the stone, begin planning the house numbers. Sketch the numbers in the center of the stone with a pencil, and then fill in the squares of each number using the sketch as a guide. Space the numbers so there are equal margins around them.

3 Place numbers

Lay out the numbers on the stepping stone using the iridized blue glass tiles. Start in the center of the stone, keeping a tile width of space between each number.

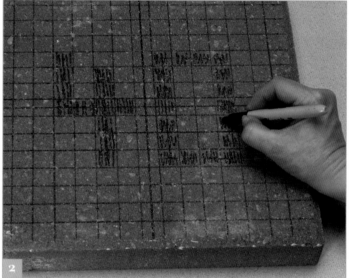

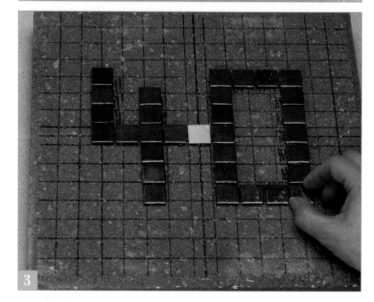

 TIP

Grids are a great help when replicating a drawing, or adding a number or letter to a tile mosaic design. The grid lines make it easy to space the design evenly or see the spacing when transferring a design.

Draw the numerals and letters on a grid, and then color in the squares to see how the mosaic will be laid out. This process assures that the spacing is consistent.

4 Place background

Fill in the background with tiles that are a different color than the numbers. For this mosaic, I used sky blue and turquoise tiles. Finish the mosaic by adding a border to the outside edge of the tile. For added interest, try to use a different pattern than what you used for the background. When you're pleased with the mosaic design, use adhesive to secure the tiles to the stone.

5 Grout and seal

Tape off the sides of the stone to keep the grout from spreading over the edges, then grout. After ten minutes, use an old towel to clean grout from the tiles. Let the grout dry completely. Once the grout is dry, remove the tape and apply sealant to the tiles.

| | | | | | | TIP | | | | | | |

A mosaic house number makes an excellent housewarming gift.

flower petal ceiling light

This project is a simple way to bring the beauty of the garden to an enclosed porch, or a guest bedroom ceiling light. A boring light shade becomes an easy project that adds an eye-catching element to your room. Change the design or colors to coordinate the shade with its surroundings. Choose glass that transmits light, then flip on the light switch and watch your project come alive!

Experiment with other garden designs in this project. Use yellow tiles for a daisy shade, or red for a rose. Or try blue and white tiles for clouds. When experimenting with designs, make sure the supporting finial in the center of the shade has enough room to screw in place to keep the shade secure.

MATERIALS AND TOOLS

- Ceiling light shade
- $^3/_8$" (10mm) iridized blue glass squares
- Blue glass nuggets
- Clear cement-based adhesive
- Tape
- Pattern PAGE 37
- Permanent black marker (optional)
- Craft knife or razor blade

1 Transfer pattern

Make a copy of the pattern found on page 37. Clean the shade using warm, soapy water. Make sure the ceiling shade is dry and clean, then attach the pattern to the inside of the shade. Press the pattern against the glass and use clear tape to keep it in place. If the lines of the pattern are still hard to see, trace over them with a permanent black marker.

2 Place border

Begin placing the glass nuggets around the edge of the shade, following the pattern lines. Secure the nuggets with adhesive, then hold them in place with tape while the adhesive dries. Next begin laying the inside circle of the pattern with the blue glass nuggets.

3 Place petals

Create the mosaic flower petals using the iridized blue glass squares, securing them with adhesive. Follow the pattern, making one loop at a time, then continuing with the loop beside it.

4 Finish petals

Continue following the pattern to fill out the design using the iridized blue glass squares.

5 Remove glue

When you finish filling out the design, remove the tape and the pattern. Clean up any adhesive that oozed from the edges of the mosaic pieces using a razor blade or a craft knife.

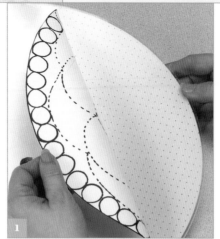

 TIP

To better see the pattern lines through the glass, press the pattern tightly to the glass and secure it in multiple locations.

■ ■ ■ enlarge the flower petal ceiling light pattern to 200% ■ ■ ■

butterfly feeder stone

This clever project is a jack-of-all-trades in disguise! Although it's certainly a gorgeous addition to any garden and is sure to be a meeting spot for butterflies, it's also a memory stone. Mount treasured keepsakes from vacations and trips in the terra-cotta concrete mix, then add a saucer for fruit and water to attract butterflies.

The terra-cotta color blends with the natural setting, but you can find many other colors of concrete mix. Use bright colors to attract butterflies. Don't limit your memory stone to just shells. Incorporate other elements, such as small figurines or bits of china. This project is a great way to showcase your treasures and invite new guests to your garden.

MATERIALS AND TOOLS

- 16" (41cm) triangular stepping stone mold
- Small terra-cotta saucer
- Rocks
- Shells or buttons
- Acrylic paint (outdoor opaque blue)
- Petroleum jelly
- Pencil
- Paintbrush
- Container
- Mixing tool

- Latex gloves
- Terra Cotta DiamondCRETE or FlashCrete
- Sealant

Note: Because the concrete product is precolored and the consistency is fine, making it easier to place the mosaic pieces, we suggest using DiamondCRETE or FlashCrete for this project. There are other concrete mixes that will work, too.

1 Label memory stone

Add a date or name you wish to commemorate to the bottom of the terra-cotta dish. Use a pencil to trace in the letters and numbers, then paint them using acrylic paint.

2 Mix concrete

Prepare the concrete mix in a container, following the directions on the package. You should mix it to the consistency of cake batter, slowly adding mix and water until you are satisfied with the results.

3 Prepare the mold

Prepare your mold by smearing the inside with petroleum jelly, then pour the concrete mix into the mold. The mix should sit just below the top of the mold. Let the mold settle for 10 minutes.

4 Begin mosaic

When the mix reaches the consistency of gelatin, you're ready to begin placing your mosaic. Start with the largest piece of the mosaic (in this case, the butterfly saucer). Set the piece on the mix, and slowly press it in place. Do not push in the piece too deeply, or it may be hidden in the mix.

TIP

When mixing concrete, it is best to start out with less water. Slowly add water and mix until it reaches the proper consistency. The measurements on the package are approximations, and you may need to make adjustments.

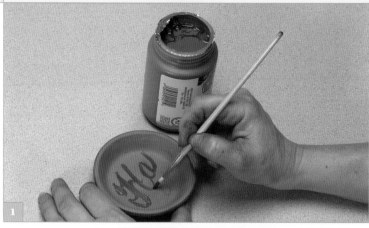

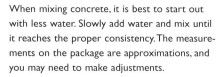

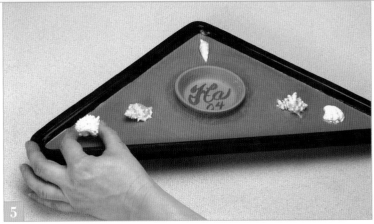

5 Place shells

Next, place your tesserae around the saucer. Start with larger items, such as shells. Try to keep a fairly even distribution of items in the mold. Work quickly, because the mix will be drying.

6 Place stones

Continue adding tesserae to the mosaic. Use smaller pieces to fill in the spaces around larger elements.

7 Add final elements

Before the mix dries, check the placement of the tesserae and add any final elements. When finished, set the mosaic aside to dry.

8 Remove from mold

Remove the mosaic from the mold after it has dried, following the setting time suggested on the concrete mix package. Once the concrete mix has fully cured, apply a sealant to the surface.

TIP

Have a basic plan for placing the tessera before you mix the concrete. You must work quickly and efficiently, because the concrete mix will be drying! If the mix becomes too dry, there's no way to remoisten it without ruining the mosaic.

birdbath saucer

The inspiration for this garden treasure is a children's poem about a turtle that swims in a puddle and climbs on rocks. Iridized glass squares sparkle in this project and glass nuggets become islands of color. The mosaic will shimmer under the sunny sky in your garden and the turtle will be a welcome guest among the flowers for years to come.

Explore other designs for this project, such as a sunflower. No matter what design you choose, this saucer will give birds a place to bathe or drink and attract the colorful guests to your garden. Pair the saucer with the Birdbath Base on page 46 for a mosaic masterpiece!

MATERIALS AND TOOLS

- Terra-cotta birdbath saucer, 14" (36cm) in diameter
- Glass nuggets
- 3/8" (10mm) glass squares in iridized green, opaque green and iridized blue
- Clear cement-based adhesive
- Adhesive tape
- Wood glue
- Water
- Pattern PAGE 45

- Paintbrush
- Small bowl
- Carbon paper and pencil
- Razor blade or craft knife
- Latex gloves
- Container
- Mixing tool
- Old towel
- Terra-cotta grout
- Sealant

1 Seal terra-cotta

Seal the entire terra-cotta saucer using a mixture of equal parts wood glue and water. Let the mixture dry.

2 Transfer pattern

Transfer the turtle pattern on page 45 to the bottom of the saucer. Use carbon paper, or draw the pattern freehand on the terra-cotta.

3 Place turtle shell

Begin laying out the glass squares and nuggets for the turtle's shell. This element will determine the spacing for the rest of the mosaic. Use alternating layers of iridized and opaque green glass squares and glass nuggets. Once you're happy with the design of the turtle's shell, use adhesive to secure the mosaic pieces in place.

4 Place border

Continue laying out the mosaic pieces for the turtle. Create a last layer around the turtle, and finish with a border of iridized blue glass squares around the edge of the saucer. Use adhesive to secure the mosaic pieces in place.

5 Place outer border

Adhere glass nuggets around the outer edge of the saucer. Use tape to hold the nuggets in place while the adhesive dries.

6 Grout and seal

Once the adhesive has set, grout the inside of the saucer using terra-cotta colored grout. After 10 minutes, clean away the excess grout using an old towel. Use a razor blade or craft knife to make sure the mosaic pieces are clean. Once the grout is completely dry, apply sealant to the mosaic.

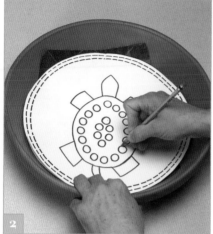

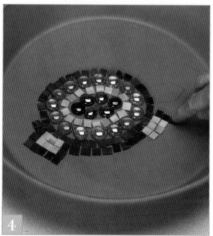

 **TIP**

Always keep a bit of extra grout for filling in any areas you missed after cleaning away the excess grout.

■ ■ ■ enlarge the birdbath saucer pattern to 179% ■ ■ ■

birdbath base

The cattails and high grasses that border ponds and lakes provide inspiration for the base of this birdbath. Iridized and opalescent glass squares sparkle, and brightly colored nuggets resemble ripe berries on a stem. As pretty as it is, you'll find the pattern is easy to adapt. Add your own elements, such as colorful flowers or butterflies.

Create this pattern on an upside-down terra-cotta pot for the base of a birdbath, or turn the pot around and use the inverted design to create your next garden storage unit. The terra-cotta pot also makes an excellent place to keep your flowers over the winter and becomes a welcome addition to any home. It's a lovely reminder of spring during the cold winter months.

MATERIALS AND TOOLS

- Large terra-cotta pot
- Glass nuggets
- 3/8" (10mm) glass squares in iridized green, opaque green and iridized blue
- Clear cement-based adhesive
- Adhesive tape
- Wood glue
- Water
- Small bowl
- Pattern PAGE 49

- Paintbrush
- Carbon paper and pencil
- Old towel
- Container
- Mixing tool
- Latex gloves
- Terra-cotta grout
- Sealant

1 Seal terra-cotta pot

Seal the entire terra-cotta pot using a paintbrush and a mixture of equal parts wood glue and water. Let the mixture dry.

2 Transfer pattern

Transfer the pattern on page 49 to the terra-cotta pot using carbon paper and a pencil, or draw the pattern freehand. The pot should sit bottom-side up, and the bottom of the pattern should sit above the lip of the pot.

3 Place glass squares

Place glass squares along the lines of the design, adhering them with adhesive. Use the iridized green, opaque green and iridized blue for the stems. To help the individual elements stand out, each plant stem in the design should have a single color.

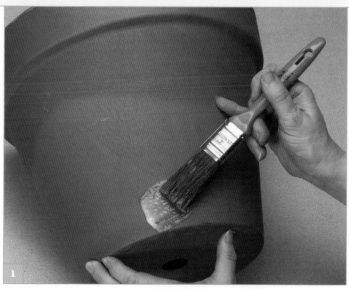

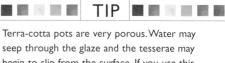

TIP

Terra-cotta pots are very porous. Water may seep through the glaze and the tesserae may begin to slip from the surface. If you use this terra-cotta pot as a planter, use a plastic liner so moisture doesn't penetrate your mosaic.

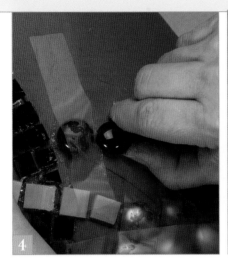

4 Place glass nuggets

Adhere the glass nuggets for the berry branches and the cattails. Tape the glass nuggets until the adhesive sets and the nuggets are secure.

5 Grout and seal

Grout to finish the mosaic. After 10 minutes, clean the grout using an old towel, making sure the grout secures the edges of the tesserae. Leave the grout only around the tesserae. Once the grout is completely dry, apply the sealant.

■ ■ ■ ■ enlarge the birdbath base pattern to 200%, enlarge to 200% again, then enlarge to 132% ■ ■ ■ ■

■ ■ ■ ■ TIP ■ ■ ■ ■

To decorate the pot right-side-up and create a planter, sketch the pattern freehand on the terra-cotta. Make sure the base of the pattern sketch sits against the bottom of the pot.

garden chime

The sound of a wind chime brings your garden to life with every breeze. Nuggets, broken china and glass bevels decorate an upside-down terra-cotta garden pot. Hang the chime in a tree, suspend it from an iron shepherd's hook in the yard, or dangle it from a hook on the porch.

This project is easy enough that a young crafter (with adult supervision) can enjoy crafting a wind chime. It's a wonderful way to spend a lazy afternoon in the garden.

MATERIALS AND TOOLS

- 4" (10cm) terra-cotta garden pot with a drainage hole (painted or plain)
- Sink strainer (Danco)
- Four beveled glass diamonds with drilled holes
- Broken glass
- Broken china SEE PAGE 14 FOR MORE INFORMATION ON SAFELY BREAKING GLASS AND CHINA FOR THIS PROJECT
- Glass nuggets
- Large bead
- 18-gauge wire

- Wood glue
- Water
- Clear cement-based adhesive
- Adhesive tape
- Small bowl
- Paintbrush
- Latex gloves
- Container
- Old towels
- White grout
- Sealant

1 Seal terra-cotta pot

Seal the terra-cotta surface of the pot with a mixture of equal parts wood glue and water. Let dry.

2 Thread wire

Thread a 16" (41cm) piece of wire through the sink strainer and up through the drainage hole in the pot. Knot a bead in the wire above the pot to secure the wire. Leave a 1½" (4cm) end on the wire above the bead to make a loop for hanging the chime.

3 Secure wires

Thread four 16" (41cm) wires through the sink strainer. Twist each wire around the sink strainer and then itself to secure the wires to the strainer. Use adhesive to secure the sink strainer to the inside of the pot. The beveled chimes will hang from these wires.

4 Place broken glass

Adhere broken glass pieces to the centers of the beveled diamonds.

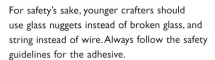

TIP

For safety's sake, younger crafters should use glass nuggets instead of broken glass, and string instead of wire. Always follow the safety guidelines for the adhesive.

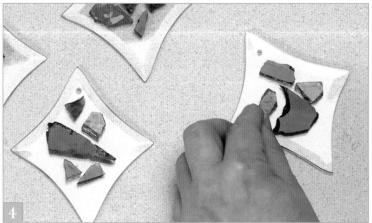

5 Place glass and broken china

Adhere glass nuggets along the top edge of the pot and broken china on the bottom. Use adhesive tape to hold the pieces in place while the glue sets. Work on a towel to keep the pot from slipping while you adhere the tesserae.

6 Grout and seal

Grout the top edge and the bottom of the pot, where you placed the tesserae. Clean the grout with an old towel after 10 minutes. Once the grout has dried completely, apply sealant.

7 Knot wires

Secure the wire inside the pot by knotting them together just below the sink strainer.

8 Hang beveled diamonds

Thread the hanging wires through the holes in the beveled diamonds. Secure the wire by wrapping it around itself above the beveled diamond. Hang the diamonds at different levels below the pot, and trim the excess wire, if necessary.

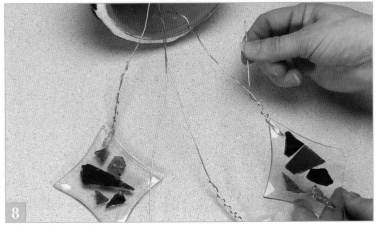

■ ■ ■ ■ **TIP** ■ ■ ■ ■

Display the wind chime once the grout has secured the tesserae. Apply the sealant later, once you're sure the grout is completely dry.

butterfly
tile

A butterfly hovering above the flowers is a welcome sight in any garden. Glass nuggets, iridized glass squares and a broken glass background combine to create this gorgeous mosaic butterfly. The contrast between the glass squares and the broken glass makes the butterfly seem to leap from the tile. Hang the tile on the wall, use it as a trivet, or place it among your potted plants.

A favorite fabric inspired this butterfly design. Search through your own favorite patterns or fabrics for inspiration. Incorporate the colors that inspire you in your mosaics. Enjoy!

MATERIALS AND TOOLS

- 8" x 8" (20cm x 20cm) tile
- Glass nuggets
- Purchase or cut ³/₈" (10mm) glass squares in red, blue, yellow and green
- Broken glass in white, off-white and brown SEE PAGE 14 FOR MORE INFORMATION ON SAFELY BREAKING GLASS FOR THIS PROJECT
- Clear cement-based adhesive
- Pattern PAGE 57

- Carbon paper and pencil
- Razor blade or craft knife
- Latex gloves
- Container
- Mixing tool
- Old towel
- Terra-cotta grout
- Sealant

1 Create pattern

Create a pattern for the tile, using either your favorite fabric as inspiration, or the pattern on page 57.

2 Transfer pattern

Transfer the pattern to the tile using carbon paper and a pencil, or use a pencil to draw the pattern on the tile freehand.

3 Place butterfly

Lay the glass squares along the lines of the butterfly's wings and body. First use red for an outline of the wings, then begin filling in yellow for the interior of the wings and blue for the body. Do not cover the areas where the glass nuggets will be placed.

4 Place nuggets

Add glass nuggets to the mosaic. If necessary, add or remove glass squares to make room for the nuggets. When you are satisfied with the butterfly, use adhesive to secure the tesserae.

5 Place background

Create the background. Lay green glass squares for the ground, then use the broken glass pieces for the sky. When you are satisfied with the placement, use adhesive to secure the tesserae. After the adhesive dries, clean away any excess adhesive using a razor blade or craft knife.

6 Grout and seal

Grout the mosaic with terra-cotta grout. After 10 minutes, clean the mosaic with an old towel. Apply sealant once the grout is completely dry.

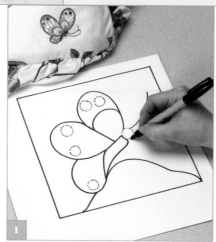

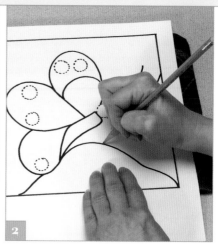

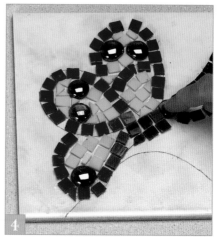

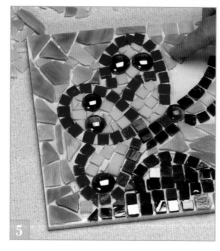

■ ■ ■ enlarge the butterfly tile pattern to 120% ■ ■ ■

■ ■ ■ ■	TIP	■ ■ ■ ■

You don't need to use broken glass for this project. Look on page 122 for a Butterfly Tile that uses only glass tiles.

catch a
falling star

Catch a falling star and put it in your garden! The border of this piece contrasts nicely with the broken-glass interior, and the bold color of the star stands out from the broken-glass background. The entire mosaic comes alive with a dark grout that highlights the colored glass. This project makes a fabulous gift to the stars in your life.

Place this stone near a light in the garden or use it as a centerpiece among the flowers that bloom in the evening. In the winter, bring the mosaic inside and prop it in a sunroom. This star will never fade away!

MATERIALS AND TOOLS

- 12" x 12" (30cm x 30cm) concrete stepping stone
- 1" x 1" (3cm x 3cm) teal tiles
- Broken glass in yellow, pink, orange, purple, cobalt blue and iridized white SEE PAGE 14 FOR MORE INFORMATION ON SAFELY BREAKING GLASS FOR THIS PROJECT
- Clear cement-based adhesive
- Masking tape
- Pattern PAGE 61
- Pencil

- Permanent black marker
- Paper
- Scissors
- Latex gloves
- Container
- Mixing tool
- Old towel
- Black grout
- Sealant

1 Lay border

Trace and cut out the star pattern on page 61. Place the star pattern in the center of the stepping stone. Lay a border of 1" (3cm) teal tiles around the edge of the stepping stone, making sure the star is still in the center. Secure the border with adhesive. When you are happy with the placement of the star, use a permanent marker to trace it on the stone.

2 Lay star

Fill in the star with orange, pink and yellow pieces of the broken glass following the pattern lines. It is easiest to start with the edges of the star, then fill in the middle. Start with larger pieces of glass, then use smaller pieces.

3 Lay background

Fill in the background with broken purple, cobalt blue and iridized white broken glass pieces. You should be using primarily the white glass pieces, adding the other colors for contrast.

4 Finish mosaic

Use the smallest tesserae to finish the background. Secure all the tesserae with adhesive.

5 Grout and seal

Tape off the stepping stone just beyond the tile border. Grout the mosaic with black grout, making sure the grout fills in all the spaces between mosaic pieces. After 10 minutes, clean off the grout with an old towel. Remove the tape and fill in gaps with extra black grout. Apply sealant when the grout is completely dry.

■ ■ ■ enlarge catch a falling star pattern to 152% ■ ■ ■

■ ■ ■ ■ TIP ■ ■ ■ ■

This simple pattern can be used many different ways. Look on page 122 for a variation of this project.

seaside garden brick

For this design, tesserae are arranged as waves and water under a setting sun. Shells washing up on shore provide a bit of reality to your mosaic, while the broken glass gives your project an artistic edge. Place the brick among potted plants or in the corner of a flowerbed or garden. You could also set it along the edge of a shed for a doorstop.

Any of your favorite scenes can become a subject for a fast, easy project such as this. A tree, a flower or an abstract design can be transferred easily to a brick. Because space is limited on the brick, this project goes quickly, but the results are impressive!

MATERIALS AND TOOLS

- Garden brick
- Broken glass in sky blue, streaky white, caramel-white, iridized cobalt blue, slate blue and yellow
  SEE PAGE 14 FOR MORE INFORMATION ON SAFELY BREAKING GLASS FOR THIS PROJECT
- Seashells
- Clear cement-based adhesive
- Pattern PAGE 65
- Carbon paper and pencil

- Latex gloves
- Container
- Mixing tool
- Old towel
- Terra-cotta grout
- Sealant

1 Transfer pattern

Make sure you are working on a clean surface and there are no cracks in the brick. Transfer the pattern on page 65 to the garden brick, either using carbon paper and a pencil or drawing freehand.

2 Lay seashells

Gather the tesserae. Place the seashells in the lower-left corner of the brick, securing them with adhesive.

3 Lay sun and sky

Lay the sun and sky pieces in the upper-left corner. Use yellow glass for the sun and blue for the sky. Secure the tesserae with adhesive when you're satisfied with the mosaic sky.

4 Continue mosaic

Continue laying tesserae across the brick. Lay the larger pieces first, then fill in with smaller pieces. Lay the dark blue water pieces in the middle of the brick and the white at the bottom.

5 Grout and seal

Grout the brick, making sure the grout fills in the space between the tesserae. Clean off the grout with an old towel after 10 minutes. Apply sealant to the mosaic once the grout is completely dry.

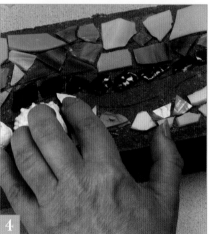

TIP

Use the naturally occuring variations in the glass you find. Look for "cloudy" pieces of glass for clouds and "wavy" glass for waves. If you have a piece of glass that really catches your attention, find a special place for it in the mosaic.

■ ■ ■ enlarge the seaside garden brick pattern to 119% ■ ■ ■

Take Another Look

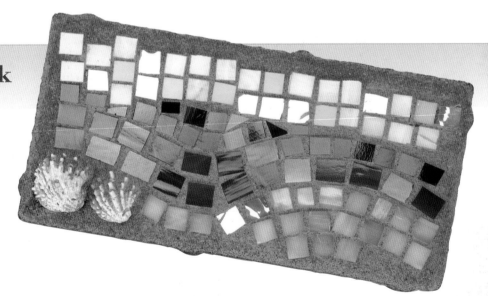

This garden brick uses purchased mosaic squares and tiles, rather than broken glass. Using purchased glass, rather than broken, makes this an excellent project for a child or a school project. Look for some interesting glass tiles, and use a found seashell from a beach trip for an unforgettable project.

garden thermometer

This groutless mosaic project isn't just a gorgeous piece of art but a useful tool as well. Surrounding a thermometer is an explosion of colorful broken glass pieces. Hang it from the wall of a shed and watch the sunlight scatter across the surface of the tile. Mirrored tiles and broken glass add modern flair to any garden setting. Or hang it next to the door to your house as a beautiful and useful greeting to guests.

If you'd rather not use broken glass for this project, purchase a mix of colorful tiles. Try other designs on the tile before you secure the tesserae. Why not add a rain catcher for your very own weather center?

MATERIALS AND TOOLS

- 12" x 12" (30cm x 30cm) ceramic tile (rough-surfaced)
- Broken glass in light blue, yellow and cobalt blue SEE PAGE 14 FOR MORE INFORMATION ON SAFELY BREAKING GLASS FOR THIS PROJECT
- ⅜" (10mm) blue and red glass squares
- Mirrored tiles
- 4" (10cm) thermometer
- Clear cement-based adhesive
- Pattern PAGE 69
- Ruler
- Carbon paper and pencil
- Razor blade

1 Place thermometer

Place the thermometer in the middle of the 12" x 12" (30cm x 30cm) tile. Find the center of the tile by drawing a line from each corner to the diagonally opposite corner. Measure out 2" (5cm) (or the radius of your thermometer) along each line from the center of the tile and make a mark. Use adhesive to secure the thermometer so the edge of the thermometer touches each mark.

2 Transfer pattern

Transfer the pattern on page 69 to the tile. Draw it freehand, or transfer it using a pencil and carbon paper.

3 Place mosaic

Apply adhesive to the glass mosaic pieces, then apply them to the tile following the pattern and surrounding the thermometer. Lay the larger tesserae first, then fill in the open areas with smaller tesserae. Mix the broken glass, mirrored tiles and glass squares.

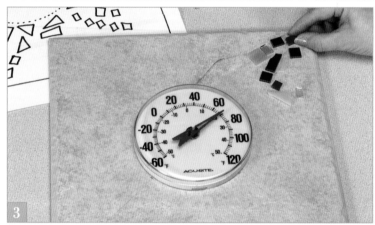

4 Clean mosaic

As you work, clean the adhesive from around the mosaic pieces using a razor blade. Fill out the pattern with tesserae until you're satisfied with results. No grout is required.

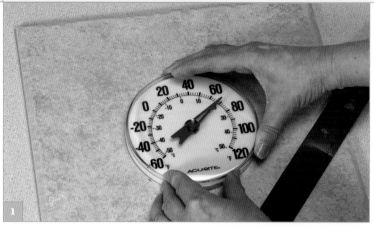

TIP

Don't feel the need to use the pattern on page 69 for this project. Explore other shapes around the thermometer. A sun shape, using yellow and red colored glass, would be appropriate. Or make a snowflake around the thermometer with iridized white and blue glass.

■ ■ ■ ■ enlarge the garden thermometer pattern to 182% ■ ■ ■ ■

■ ■ ■ ■ **TIP** ■ ■ ■ ■

Tiles make an excellent surface
for mosaic projects. Not only
are they flat, they come in a
variety of textures and colors.

country clock

Craft a new look for an old object with this quick, easy project. Add broken china and glass nuggets to the border or base of a simple clock, then add grout for a project that is sure to attract attention and admirers. Inspired by the shabby charm of the garden, this project is a perfect addition to a porch, sunroom or kitchen.

With the fabulous selection of china and glass nuggets as well as a wide selection of colored grouts, there's no limit to the variations. Design the mosaic to match your décor, or plan an entire theme room around the project.

MATERIALS AND TOOLS

- Purchased clock, with an outer frame, from garden store or flea market (Garden Treasures #219274)
- Broken china SEE PAGE 14 FOR MORE INFORMATION ON SAFELY BREAKING CHINA FOR THIS PROJECT
- Glass nuggets
- Adhesive paper
- Clear cement-based adhesive
- Scissors

- Latex gloves
- Container
- Mixing tool
- Old towel
- Screwdriver or flat tool
- White grout
- Sealant

1 Protect clock

Protect the clock face by covering it with a piece of adhesive paper. Make sure to trim the adhesive paper so it covers only the clock face.

2 Begin mosaic

Apply glass nuggets and broken china to the outside frame of the clock. Intersperse the glass nuggets around the broken china. Start with the larger broken china pieces.

3 Finish mosaic

Apply smaller broken china pieces in the open spaces.

4 Check frame

Take a last look at the completed frame, making sure there are no open areas and the tesserae is fairly level so the mosaic won't be buried under the grout. Add or remove any pieces until you are satisfied with the results, then use adhesive to secure the tesserae to the frame.

5 Grout clock

Grout the frame of the clock. Make sure to cover the space around the mosaic pieces completely.

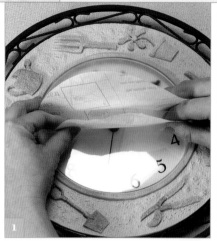

■ ■ ■ ■ ■ ■ TIP ■ ■ ■ ■ ■ ■

Be careful when cleaning the grout from the frame of the clock. Broken china may have sharp edges, which will be hidden beneath the grout.

6 Clean grout

Use an old towel to clean the grout from the china pieces and glass nuggets after 10 minutes. Expose the top of the mosaic pieces from the grout. The grout may cover some of the smaller mosaic pieces, so you may need to chisel some of the grout away from the top of the tesserae with a screwdriver or other flat tool.

7 Remove adhesive paper

Carefully remove the adhesive paper, making sure it doesn't remove any mosaic pieces or grout. Repair any imperfections, then apply sealant to the mosaic once the grout has completely dried.

Take Another Look

Using a darker-colored grout will better highlight the clock and help bring out the colors in the broken china and glass nuggets. Why not use the colors in the room where the clock will be displayed as inspiration?

sailor's
delight

In this delightful scene, a sailboat rests on an ocean of iridized white and blue. Glass nugget treasures hide on the ocean floor. Broken glass pieces are arranged on a purchased stepping-stone and then highlighted with colored grout. This project would look perfect amid flowers or sitting beside a pond framed with reeds and lily pads. The choice of colors will help bring out the colors of your garden flowers.

You can work this project with glass tiles or shaped glass pieces as easily as the broken glass pieces. And with a multitude of acrylic paint colors on the market, you won't lack for a choice of colors for the grout. Spend some time in your garden exploring different color combinations before working on this mosaic. It's the perfect excuse to enjoy a day outdoors!

MATERIALS AND TOOLS

- 12" (30cm) round stepping stone
- Broken glass pieces in iridized streaky white, streaky red, streaky yellow, opaque blue and streaky pink SEE PAGE 14 FOR MORE INFORMATION ON SAFELY BREAKING GLASS FOR THIS PROJECT
- Glass nuggets
- Clear cement-based adhesive
- Pattern PAGE 77
- Carbon paper and pencil

- Old towel
- Latex gloves
- Container
- Mixing tool
- Acrylic paint: Purple Dusk (Delta)
- White grout
- Sealant

1 Transfer pattern

Transfer the pattern on page 77 to the stepping-stone using carbon paper or by drawing it freehand on the surface.

2 Begin mosaic

Start the mosaic by using yellow glass to place the sun. Follow the lines of the sun, then fill in the interior. Use larger pieces first, then fill in the space with smaller pieces. Secure the tesserae with adhesive.

3 Continue mosaic

Continue the mosaic, moving down the stone and laying one color at a time. Fill in a section, following the colors on the final project, or use your own colors. Once you're satisfied with a section, secure the tesserae with adhesive and move onto the next.

4 Add glass nuggets

Add glass nuggets at the bottom of the mosaic once you have the broken glass pieces in position. Secure the nuggets with adhesive.

5 Color grout

Mix white grout as you normally would. For an added effect, mix acrylic paint with the grout. Start with a little paint and mix. Keep adding paint until you're satisfied with the color of the grout.

6 Grout and seal

Grout the mosaic, making sure the grout has penetrated all the cracks between mosaic pieces. After 10 minutes, clean off the grout with an old towel. Apply sealant once the grout is completely dry.

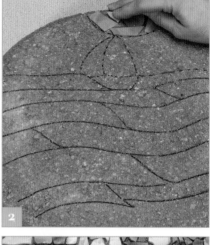

■ ■ ■ enlarge the sailor's delight pattern to 179% ■ ■ ■

■ ■ ■ ■ TIP ■ ■ ■ ■

You can use this pattern to make cut-glass pieces for the mosaic. Take a look at a cut glass version of this project on page 124.

stained glass flower

Sometimes the prettiest color combinations are found while rummaging through glass and china scraps. The glass in this mosaic is the leftovers from previous projects. The inspiration for this project came from the colors you find in gorgeous art deco stained glass windows. Variations of green added to the variety of reds, highlighted with a black grout background that resembles lead in a stained glass window, make the colors vibrant.

Select other easy patterns and spice them up with recycled tessera. Create your mosaic on a purchased stepping-stone, which come in a variety of shapes and sizes. In this project, you'll also learn a new way to secure your tesserae. In no time you can fill your garden with beautiful garden stones!

MATERIALS AND TOOLS

- 12" (30cm) circular stepping stone
- Broken glass pieces (scraps from other projects) in red, orange, lime green, blue green, purple, cobalt blue, turquoise, white, iridized white and teal SEE PAGE 14 FOR MORE INFORMATION ON SAFELY BREAKING GLASS FOR THIS PROJECT
- Clear cement-based adhesive
- Pattern PAGE 81
- Carbon paper and pencil

- Latex gloves
- Large container
- Mixing tool
- Old towel
- Razor blade (optional)
- Black grout
- Sealant

1 Transfer pattern

Transfer the pattern on page 81 to the stepping-stone using carbon paper or by drawing it freehand on the surface.

2 Begin mosaic

Begin laying out the mosaic using the tesserae. Start with the flower. Once you have a section complete, move aside the pieces and smear adhesive over the stone's surface. Place the mosaic pieces back in position, working quickly. Once you have the flower complete, move on to the next section of the design. Note: Make sure there is at least ⅛" (3mm) space between the tesserae.

3 Continue mosaic

Start laying out the background. Continue laying out the broken glass one section at a time. Remove the glass and spread the adhesive directly on the stone's surface, then place the glass back on the adhesive-covered surface. Continue until the mosaic is complete.

4 Finish mosaic

Use a pencil or razor blade to clear the space around each piece of tesserae. The black grout needs to surround the tesserae to give the mosaic the appearance of stained glass.

5 Grout and seal

Mix up black grout in a container and apply to the mosaic. After 10 minutes, clean the mosaic using an old towel. When the grout is completely dry, apply sealant.

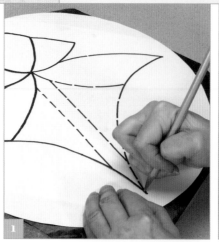

TIP

The inspiration for this mosaic came from a stained glass window. Look for inspiration in artwork you admire, such as paintings. Find color combinations and patterns for your mosaics in the world around you. Flower beds are an excellent place to search for inspiration.

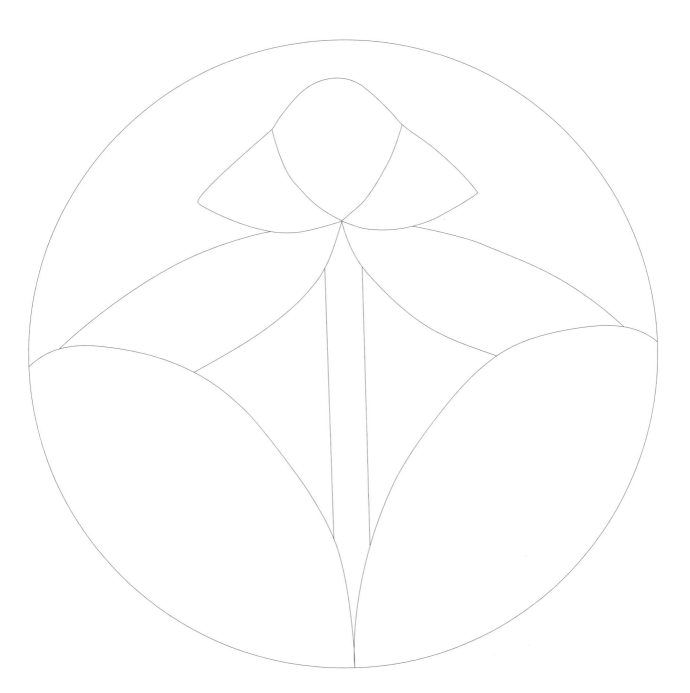

■ ■ ■ enlarge the stained glass flower pattern to 182% ■ ■ ■

garden tabletop

This tabletop mosaic project is both gorgeous and unique. With a bit of imagination, you can see rays of sunlight in a blue sky, with a meandering creek flowing down a rocky hillside into a glittering lake. Abstract landscapes such as this are easy to create. Sketch out a design, then use broken glass pieces to fill in sections that follow the lines of the design. Let your imagination run wild with this projects.

Tabletops are excellent surfaces for a mosaic. Using the indirect method to create the mosaic keeps the top flat. The stepping stone mold fits nicely on an iron garden table, though you should make sure the stone is secure in the table base. Many other materials, such as glass or wood, can be used as a surface for tabletop mosaics.

MATERIALS AND TOOLS

- 14" (36cm) round stepping stone mold
- 2" x 2" (5cm x 5cm) ceramic tiles
- Random broken glass and china pieces SEE PAGE 14 FOR MORE INFORMATION ON SAFELY BREAKING GLASS FOR THIS PROJECT
- Adhesive paper
- Pattern PAGE 85
- Paper
- Pencil
- Scissors

- Latex gloves
- Container
- Mixing tool
- Petroleum jelly
- Coat hanger
- Wire cutters
- Old towel
- Putty knife (optional)
- Concrete mix
- Sealant

1 Create pattern

Make two copies of the pattern on page 85. Lay a tile border on one copy of the pattern.

2 Place mosaic

Use broken glass and china pieces to fill in the pattern, following the color pattern of the final project found on page 82. Don't worry about keeping the shapes exact. Just use the pattern as a guide.

3 Prepare mold

When you're satisfied with the mosaic, prepare the mold. Smear the inside of the mold with petroleum jelly. Using a light box or a sunny window and the other pattern copy, trace the pattern on the back so it is on both sides of the paper. The version on the back will be in reverse. Lay the pattern facedown in the mold. Trim the adhesive sheet to fit the mold, then remove the backing and lay it, sticky side up, on the pattern. Transfer all the mosaic pieces from your previous pattern to the one in the mold, adhering them to the adhesive sheet.

4 Add concrete

Mix the concrete and pour it in the prepared mold and over the mosaic pieces. Fill the mold halfway to the top.

5 Embed coat hanger

Settle and level the concrete mix in the mold. Embed pieces of wire, such as a bent coat hanger, into the concrete mix. Lay them flat. The wire shouldn't extend beyond the concrete. If necessary, trim the wire. These wires will lend support to the finished piece.

6 Finish mosaic

Finish pouring and settle the concrete in the mold. Allow to dry. When the concrete is dry, remove the mosaic from the mold. Pull away the adhesive paper and clean the mosaic with an old towel and a putty knife. Apply sealant when the concrete has fully cured.

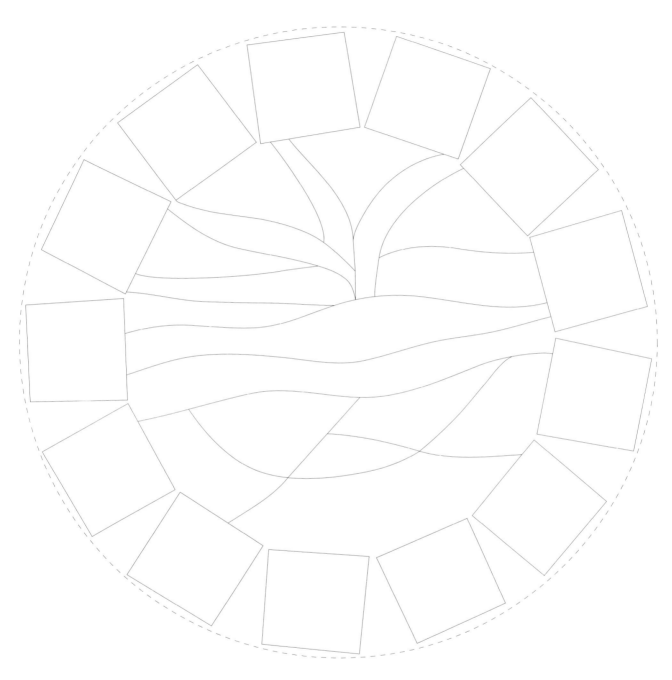

■ ■ ■ ■ enlarge the garden tabletop pattern to 189% ■ ■ ■ ■

■ ■ ■ ■ ■ ■ **TIP** ■ ■ ■ ■ ■ ■

There's no need to be exact when working on this mosaic. Explore different colors or shapes before pouring the concrete. Find a combination that is pleasing to you. Who knows what you'll come up with?

blooming daisies garden stone

Glass petals, broken china and flat stones are combined on a garden stone for a project that is sure to brighten any spot in the garden. Place this stone among a patch of ivy or your favorite flowers, or lean it against an old urn or birdbath. It also makes an excellent gift for someone who is just starting his or her own garden.

For this project you'll have the chance to cut petals from glass, or you could use broken glass or purchase precut glass petals. Broken china and decorative flat stones add to the design. Combining all these elements creates a project that is both beautiful and fun.

MATERIALS AND TOOLS

- 12" x 12" (30cm x 30cm) concrete stepping stone
- Flat, purchased decorative stones, attached to mesh
- Glass nuggets
- Cut glass petal shapes from opaque and streaky orange and yellow glass
- Opaque and streaky green glass rectangles
- Green purchased stones
- Broken china SEE PAGE 14 FOR MORE INFORMATION ON SAFELY BREAKING CHINA FOR THIS PROJECT
- Clear cement-based adhesive

- Spray adhesive
- Pattern PAGE 89
- Carbon paper and pencil or permanent black marker
- Glass cutter
- Grozing pliers
- Running pliers
- Electric glass grinder
- Container
- Mixing tool
- Latex gloves
- Old towel
- Black grout
- Sealant

1 Transfer pattern

Cut out the petal pieces from the pattern and place them on the orange and yellow glass. Cut out the petals from the glass, following the directions for cutting glass on page 15. Place, then trace the cut-glass flowers on the surface. Transfer the rest of the pattern on page 89 to the stepping-stone using carbon paper or by drawing freehand it on the surface.

2 Place decorative stones

Place the flat, decorative stones, still attached to the mesh, at the bottom of the stepping stone. Use adhesive to secure the stones and mesh to the stepping stone.

3 Place petals and grass

Following the pattern, place the petals at the top of the stone. Use glass nuggets for the centers of the flowers. Place the green glass and green decorative stones as grass and stems for the flowers. Secure the tesserae with adhesive.

4 Place broken china

Place broken china in the area between the green grass and stems and the flat, decorative stones. Leave at least a ⅛" (3mm) space between each piece of china. Use adhesive to secure the china.

5 Grout

Grout the mosaic, making sure the grout fills the space between the tesserae. Bevel the edge of the grout on the stone. Let the grout set for 10 minutes.

6 Clean and seal

Clean the grout from the mosaic using an old towel. Use a putty knife to clean the grout from the top of the china. You may need to scrub the grout from the flat pieces, and pick at the grout in the rough edges of the china. Apply sealant when the grout is completely dry.

TIP

A glass grinder isn't necessary if you make clean breaks when you cut your glass petals.

■ ▨ ▨ ▨ enlarge the blooming daisies garden stone pattern to 182% ▨ ▨ ▨ ▨

fish fountain

Fountains are the perfect addition to gardens, both indoors and out. The soothing sound of flowing water helps block the noise of a hectic world and gives the space an aura of tranquility. The floor of this ocean mosaic scene is colored with coral and sand. Brightly colored fish swim above. Water flowing over your creation adds a new element to your mosaic as the fish shimmer and sparkle.

Secure this mosaic to a piece of glass and add a dark grout for contrast that will dazzle in the water. Most fountains can become a base for the mosaic. Create your own underwater scene, or find inspiration elsewhere in nature, such as a rainbow or a rainforest scene.

MATERIALS AND TOOLS

- Tabletop fountain (EnviraScape waterfall by HoMedics)
- Window glass
- Art glass in red, purple, yellow, orange and slate blue
- Cobalt blue glass nuggets
- Spray adhesive
- Clear cement-based adhesive (water-resistant)
- Pattern PAGE 93
- Glass cutter
- Grozing pliers
- Running pliers
- Glass nippers
- Wire cutters
- Electric glass grinder or drill
- 1/8" (3mm) bit
- Latex gloves
- Container
- Mixing tool
- Old towel
- 16-gauge wire
- Pliers
- Black grout (water-resistant)
- Sealant

1 Cut window glass

Cut a piece of window glass to fit the fountain. The glass for this fountain is 6½" x 10" (17cm x 25cm). Drill holes in the upper-left and-right corners of the window glass with a glass grinder and a ⅛" (3mm) bit. Cut out the fish and seashell glass pieces for the mosaic using the patterns found on page 93 and following the instructions on page 15. Cut ½" (13mm) squares from the purple and slate blue glass for the background.

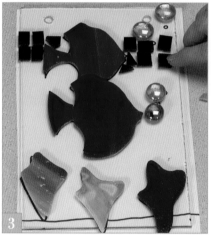
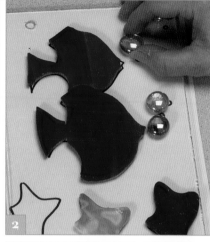
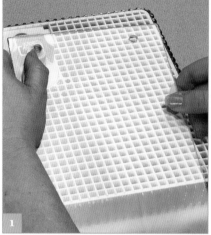

2 Place cut glass

Lay the pattern beneath the cut window glass. Begin adding the mosaic pieces to the top of the glass, following the pattern. First add the cut-glass shapes and the glass nuggets. Secure the tesserae using the adhesive.

3 Place background

Once you have the cut-glass shapes secured, begin filling in the background with mosaic squares. You may wish to use glass nippers to trim some of the squares to more closely fit the curves of the cut glass shapes. Use lines of yellow and orange glass for the top and bottom of the mosaic, then make rows of purple and slate blue glass for the background.

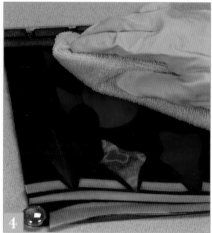

4 Grout and seal

When you are satisfied, grout the mosaic with black grout. After 10 minutes, clean the mosaic with an old towel. Once the grout is completely dry, apply sealant.

5 Assemble fountain

Using the holes you made in step 1, attach the mosaic to the tabletop fountain with pieces of wire. Wind the wire around the brass top of the fountain, so that water will run over the mosaic. Trim the excess wire, or twist it for a decorative effect.

■ ■ ■ enlarge the fish fountain pattern to 154% ■ ■ ■

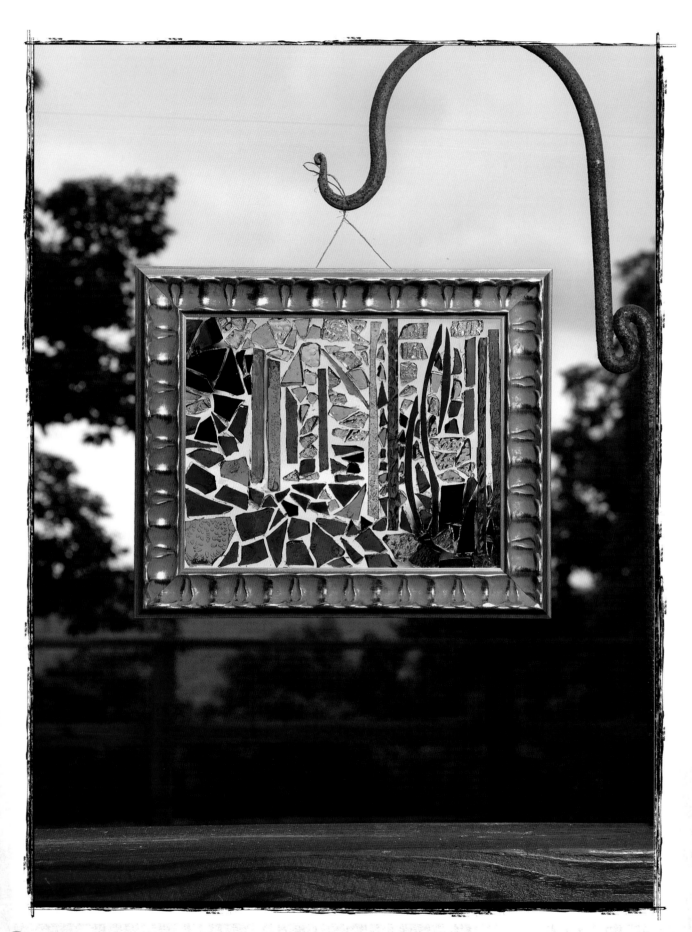

landscape photo

Can you tell that the design for this groutless mosaic project came from a favorite forest photograph? Combine gorgeous inspiration, a fabulous decorative frame and beautiful glass and you'll have an eye-catching mosaic that brings a bit of the woods to any room in the house. Let light fall on this project and watch it play across the glass.

Using large glass pieces to follow the colorful landscape, you could create an abstract mosaic. Using smaller pieces of shaped colored glass will create a more realistic mosaic. No matter what you do, the results of this project are bound to be alluring. Hang your project in a window for the best effect.

MATERIALS AND TOOLS

- 10" x 10" (25cm x 25cm) picture frame with glass
- Art Glass in colors matching the photograph (for this photo we used cathedral blue, cathedral green, brown granite, cathedral orange and cathedral red)
- Clear cement-based adhesive
- Clear silicone
- 8" x 10" (20cm x 25cm) color photograph or use the photograph on page 97

- Color copier (optional)
- Glass cutter
- Grozing pliers
- Running pliers
- Glass nippers
- Electric glass grinder
- Razor blade

1 Secure glass

Remove the backing from the picture frame, then secure the glass to the frame with clear silicone. Do not let the silicone seep beyond the edge of the frame.

2 Place photograph

Place your color photograph (or the one on page 97) beneath the glass. The photo should be centered under the glass with the edge of the photo and the edge of the glass aligned.

3 Place cut glass

Look for straight lines in the photo, and cut pieces of colored glass that match the straight lines (such as tree trunks or flower stems). Begin laying the cut, straight pieces in place on top of the glass and over the matching areas of the photo. Do not secure these pieces yet.

4 Begin mosaic

Begin laying the random broken glass tesserae in one corner. Fill an area with a single color of glass before moving to the next area and color. Don't try to be too exact while filling in the details. Use broad areas of general color, rather than focusing on exact details.

5 Continue mosaic

Continue laying the broken tesserae on the glass, following the edge of the frame and filling in a single area of color before moving to the next. As you finish the edge, move toward the middle of the glass.

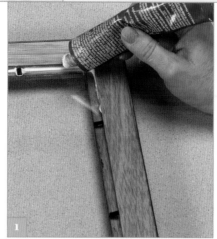

TIP

If you wish to use your own photo for this project and it's not the right size for your frame, size the copy using a color copier.

6 Finish mosaic

Finish laying the colored, broken glass in the mosaic. Use smaller pieces to fill in empty areas, being careful not to knock the previous pieces you've laid out of position.

7 Secure glass

When you're satisfied with the mosaic, secure all the tesserae to the glass using the adhesive. Make adjustments to the mosaic as you work. Use a razor blade to clean up any excess adhesive, then allow the adhesive to dry.

■ ■ ■ enlarge the original landscape photo pattern to 167% ■ ■ ■

tulips garden stone

Beautiful glass tulips climb their way up this stepping stone. A background of iridescent white rectangles holds the elegant tulips. Follow the simple pattern, or let your imagination explore new arrangements.

For this project, you'll learn how to make your own rectangles for the background. We use white rectangles for this project, but why not use the colors in your own garden? Place the garden stone near the tulips, and with your clever use of colored glass, the stone will complement the flowers beautifully! This project also makes an excellent gift for anyone with a love for the garden.

MATERIALS AND TOOLS

- 6" x 16" (15cm x 41cm) rectangular stepping stone mold
- Glass in opaque yellow, opaque orange and opaque green
- Iridized white glass squares (purchased or cut into rectangles)
- Spray adhesive
- Adhesive paper
- Adhesive tape
- Pattern PAGE 101
- Ruler
- Scissors or mosaic shears
- Glass cutter
- Grozing pliers
- Running pliers
- Electric glass grinder
- Latex gloves
- Container
- Mixing tool
- Petroleum jelly
- Hammer
- Paint scraper
- Old towel
- Concrete mix
- Grout: concrete (optional)
- Sealant

1 Prepare glass

Cut out glass squares for the background of your tulip. Start by cutting ½" (1cm) strips of the iridized white glass.

2 Cut glass

Cut the strips of iridized white glass into 1" (3cm) rectangles, breaking off the pieces as you go.

3 Begin mosaic

Make two copies of the pattern. Cut out the yellow, orange and green shaped glass pieces using one of the pattern copies and following the instructions on page 15. Prepare the mold with petroleum jelly. Using a light box or a sunny window, trace the pattern onto the back of the other copy. Lay this pattern in the mold. Trim an adhesive sheet to fit the pattern, then remove the backing and lay it, sticky side up, on the pattern. Use tape to hold these pieces together. Following the pattern, place the cut-glass tulip pieces on the adhesive sheet.

4 Place background

Place the cut rectangle pieces around the flower pattern for the background.

5 Pour concrete

Following directions on the package, mix concrete in a container. Pour the concrete to the very top of the mold. Settle the concrete, and then let dry.

6 Seal mosaic

When dry, remove the mosaic from the mold. Using a paint scraper, repair imperfections in the concrete with a similarly colored grout. Apply sealant when the grout or concrete has fully cured.

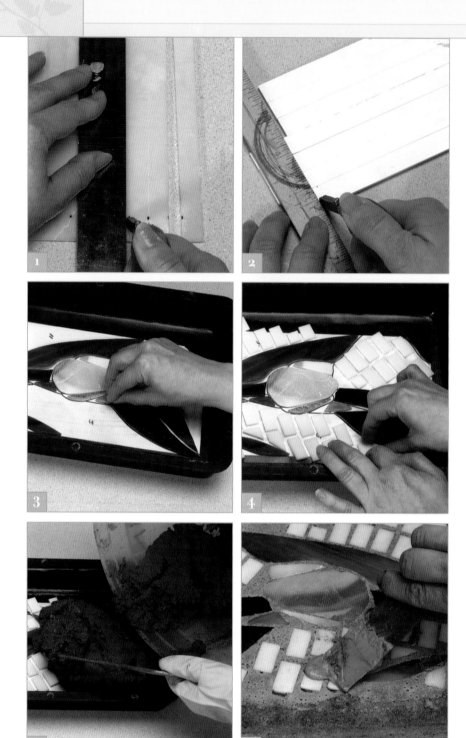

■ ■ ■ ■ ■ **TIP** ■ ■ ■ ■ ■ ■

When cutting many squares or rectangles from glass, try using the width of a ruler or a piece of wood as a template rather than measuring each piece. This will keep the squares more consistent and make your job much easier.

enlarge the tulips garden stone pattern to 182%

bunny
plaque

Is your garden a place that's filled with fond memories? This project takes that idea to a whole new level. What child wouldn't be proud to see his or her work become an everlasting garden stone or a plaque that decorates a porch, arbor or any room in the house? I hope my daughter appreciates seeing her third-grade artwork again after all these years. This is an excellent gift for a parent or grandparent—a child's favorite drawing created in stone!

Begin with a simple drawing and use that as the pattern. Random squares fill in the background of the mosaic. Try to capture the personality of the work, rather than the exact drawing. Remain true to the colors of the child's painting as well as the shapes.

MATERIALS AND TOOLS

- 6" x 16" (15cm x 41cm) rectangular stepping-stone mold
- Two eye hooks (optional)
- Glass: opaque white, opaque purple, opaque pink and opaque green
- Spray adhesive
- Adhesive paper
- Adhesive tape
- Pattern PAGE 105 OR CREATE YOUR OWN
- Child's drawing (optional)
- Pencil
- Paper
- Scissors or mosaic shears
- Glass cutter

- Grozing pliers
- Running pliers
- Electric glass grinder
- Glass nippers
- Latex gloves
- Container
- Mixing tool
- Old towel
- Petroleum jelly
- Paint scraper
- Ivory or off-white DiamondCRETE or FlashCrete
- Sealant

1 Create pattern

Create a pattern from a child's drawing, or use the one on page 105. Trace the drawing on a piece of paper, then trace the interior shapes, making sure all the lines extend to the edge of the pattern. Use only complete shapes.

2 Cut glass

Make two copies of the pattern. Use one copy to cut the glass shapes using the appropriately colored glass and following the instructions for cutting glass on page 15. Place the shaped glass on the other pattern, making sure the pieces fit and there is room between pieces for the concrete to secure the tesserae. Make adjustments as necessary. Cut ¾" (19mm) squares of opaque purple glass for the background.

3 Begin mosaic

Prepare the mold with petroleum jelly. Using a light box or a sunny window and the other copy of the pattern, trace the pattern on the back of the paper so it appears in reverse. Lay the pattern facedown in the mold. Trim an adhesive sheet to fit the pattern, then remove the backing from the sheet and lay it, sticky side up, on the pattern. Begin placing the cut-glass pieces in the mold.

4 Finish mosaic

Lay a background of opaque purple glass squares. When finished, mix and pour the concrete. Pour less for a wall hanging and more for a stepping stone. If desired, place eye hooks in the concrete near the top of the mold. Allow the concrete to dry to the consistency of gelatin before you add the eye hooks.

5 Clean and seal

When the concrete is dry, remove the mosaic from the mold and clean it. Apply sealant once the concrete has completely set.

6 Eye hooks

If you want to hang the mosaic, use adhesive to secure the eye hooks in the concrete.

■ ■ ■ ■ enlarge the bunny plaque pattern to 182% ■ ■ ■ ■

summer
poppies

There is nothing more enchanting than a field of poppies in the summer. Red, yellow and orange petals surrounded with wispy green leaves and fuzzy purple balls waiting to become blossoms.

These flower shapes are the perfect theme for a picture or a long, narrow backsplash for a sink or stovetop. An art glass supplier can provide a custom-sized stained glass wooden frame that will hold a piece of window glass as a surface. For a larger piece, one that could be used as a backsplash in the kitchen, repeat this pattern or trace the flowers randomly in order to expand the design. It's bound to be the highlight of a kitchen or bath and a lovely reminder of your garden.

MATERIALS AND TOOLS

- 10" x 16" (25cm x 41cm) stained glass wooden frame
- Window glass to fit the frame
- Glass (mottled with variegated colors) in pink, red, orange, yellow, slate blue, gold and green
- Clear silicone
- Clear cement-based adhesive
- Spray adhesive
- Adhesive tape
- Glass cleaner
- Acrylic paint: red (optional)
- Paintbrush (optional)
- Pattern PAGE 109

- Scissors or mosaic shears
- Glass cutter
- Grozing pliers
- Running pliers
- Glass nippers
- Electric glass grinder
- Latex gloves
- Container
- Mixing tool
- Paint scraper or razor blade
- Old towel
- Black grout
- Sealant

1 Secure glass

If desired, paint the frame red, then assemble the frame. Secure the window glass to the frame with silicone. Try to keep the silicone from seeping beyond the edge of the frame.

2 Cut glass pieces

Make two copies of the pattern on page 109. Cut out the glass pieces from appropriately colored glass using one pattern and following the instructions on page 15. Assemble the cut glass on the other pattern to check the size and shape of the pieces. Use the glass grinder to make adjustments as necessary.

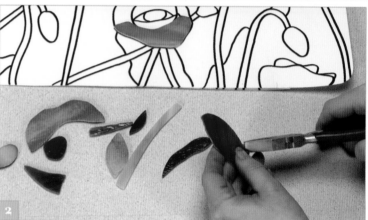

3 Place pattern

Secure the other pattern behind the glass using adhesive tape. Center the pattern near the bottom. The pattern shouldn't touch the top of the frame. The area above the flowers will be covered by the background tesserae.

4 Begin mosaic

Make sure the glass is very clean before you begin. Using adhesive, secure the cut-glass pieces to the front of the window glass, using the pattern as your guide.

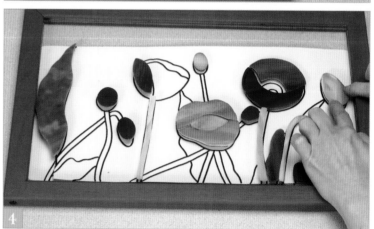

 TIP

For a pattern such as this, which requires more elaborate cuts, you may want to use glass pieces larger than those indicated by the pattern. For example, use a single piece of glass for a flower. The shadings will suggest petals. This way you won't need to make as many cuts.

5 Place background

Using glass squares or tiles, place the slate blue background around the cut glass pieces. Lay the larger pieces first, then lay smaller pieces in the open areas. Secure the tesserae with adhesive.

6 Grout and seal

When the adhesive is dry, clear away any excess with a paint scraper or razor blade, then grout the mosaic. Try to keep the grout off the frame. After 10 minutes, clean the mosaic using an old towel. Apply sealant once the grout is completely dry.

▩ ▩ ▩ enlarge the summer poppies pattern to 200%, then enlarge to 116% ▩ ▩ ▩

▩ ▩ ▩ **TIP** ▩ ▩ ▩

See page 123 for a version of this project that would work as a kitchen backsplash.

seaside village garden stone

The sun, warm weather, sandy beaches and coastal towns inspired this garden stone. Blue colorant, added to the concrete, suggests the color of the sea and sky in this project. Place it in the corner of the garden or in a flower bed, or use it to showcase some found treasures from a special vacation spot.

Any stepping stone mold can be adapted to this pattern. Simply place the houses in the mold, maintaining a space around the edges. Add more shapes to the mold, or create new ones in the pattern to make this village an achitectural wonder all your own.

MATERIALS AND TOOLS

- Garden border stepping stone mold
- Glass in opaque red, opaque yellow, opaque blue, opaque brown and opaque orange
- Glass nuggets
- Shells
- Spray adhesive
- Adhesive paper
- Adhesive tape
- Clear cement-based adhesive
- Pattern PAGE 113
- Scissors
- Petroleum jelly
- Glass cutter

- Grozing pliers
- Running pliers
- Glass nippers
- Electric glass grinder
- Latex gloves
- Container
- Mixing tool
- Craft foam (or a thicker foam product)
- Old towel
- Brass wire brush or paint scraper
- Concrete
- Blue colorant (such as acrylic paint or concrete colorant)
- Sealant

1 Create mosaic

Create two copies of the pattern on page 113. Use one of the patterns to cut out glass pieces for the mosaic, following the instructions on page 15. Assemble the cut-glass pieces on the original pattern to check spacing. Using a light box or a sunny window, trace the pattern onto the back of the other pattern copy. Prepare the mold with petroleum jelly, then lay the pattern facedown in the mold. Trim an adhesive sheet to the size of the pattern, then remove the backing from the sheet and lay it, sticky side up, on the pattern. Use tape to hold these pieces together. Add the cut-glass elements to the pattern in the mold.

2 Add dimensional elements

For any dimensional elements of the design, such as seashells or glass nuggets, cut out a piece of craft foam of a similar size and add it to the design. Place the foam on the adhesive paper. This will create a space in the concrete that you can later use to add in the dimensional element itself.

3 Mix concrete

Mix concrete for the mold in a container. Add blue colorant to the mix. If you would like a deeper shade of blue, add more colorant. Add less for a lighter shade.

4 Pour concrete

Pour the concrete into the mold. Settle the concrete and then let dry.

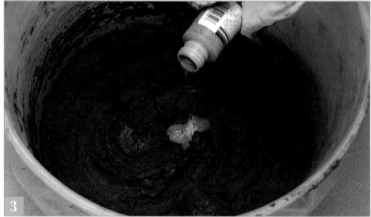

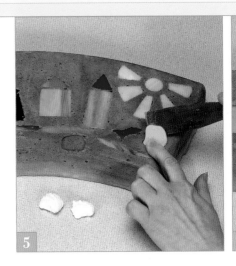

5 Remove foam

Remove the concrete from the mold when it is dry and clean the mosaic with an old towel, paint scraper or brass wire brush. Carefully remove the foam pieces from the concrete using a paint scraper.

6 Place three-dimensional elements

Use adhesive to glue the dimensional elements to the mosaic where the foam pieces were. Apply sealant once the concrete is completely set.

■ ▦ ▨ enlarge the seaside village garden stone pattern to 200%, then enlarge to 125% ▨ ▦ ■

coneflower garden stone

This small garden stone is the perfect gift for your favorite gardener. With an iridized, sky blue background that sets off the contrasting leaves, stem and petals, this square stone imitates a coneflower in full color and form. The cut-glass shapes give this project an artistic look. Placed among the bushes or in a garden border, this flower blooms when others have faded.

This project makes a big impact, but little time is spent in construction. With a project so small, the choice of beautiful glass is important. The contrasting colors and textures are what make this design so striking. If you find a glass or material you love, design a mosaic around it. Try to highlight what you love about the glass, such as the color or pattern, in the design.

MATERIALS AND TOOLS

- 8" (20cm) square stepping stone mold
- Glass in opaque orange, opaque leaf green, light green, iridized light blue and iridized amber
- Spray adhesive
- Adhesive paper
- Adhesive tape
- Pattern PAGE 117
- Scissors or mosaic shears
- Petroleum jelly
- Glass cutter

- Grozing pliers
- Running pliers
- Electric glass grinder
- Latex gloves
- Container
- Mixing tool
- Hammer
- Old towel
- Putty knife
- Concrete
- Sealant

1 Cut pattern

Make two copies of the pattern on page 117. Use one of the copies to cut glass pieces for the mosaic following the instructions on page 15. Assemble the cut-glass pieces on the other copy of the pattern to make sure the pieces fit. Make adjustments as necessary using the electric glass grinder.

2 Prepare mold

Prepare the mold with petroleum jelly. Using a light box or a sunny window and the other pattern, trace the pattern onto the back side of the paper. Lay the pattern facedown in the mold. Trim an adhesive sheet to fit the pattern, then remove the backing from the sheet and lay it, sticky side up, on the pattern. Use tape to hold these pieces together.

3 Place mosaic

Lay the glass pieces on the adhesive paper, using the pattern as a guide.

4 Pour concrete

When the mosaic is complete, mix concrete and pour it in the mold. Make sure the concrete settles between all the mosaic pieces.

5 Settle concrete

Gently tap the side of the mold with the hammer after you place the concrete. This will help make sure the concrete settles between the mosaic pieces. When finished, set the mosaic aside to dry.

6 Apply sealant

Carefully remove the mosaic from the mold when the concrete is dry. Use an old towel or a putty knife to clean the concrete. Apply sealant once the concrete has completely set.

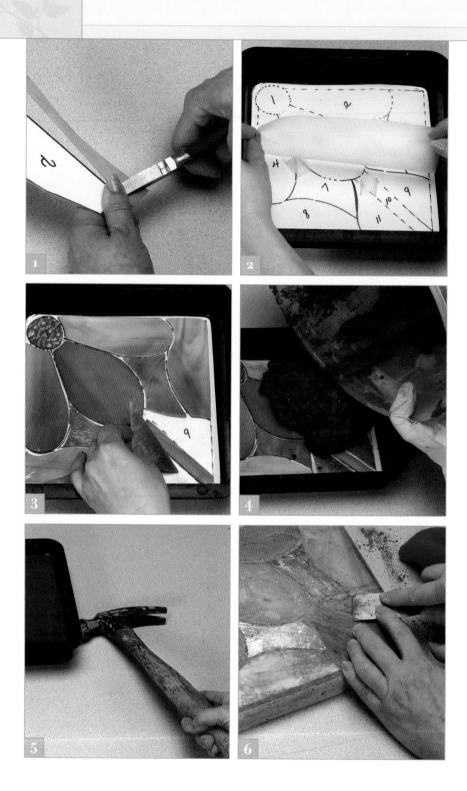

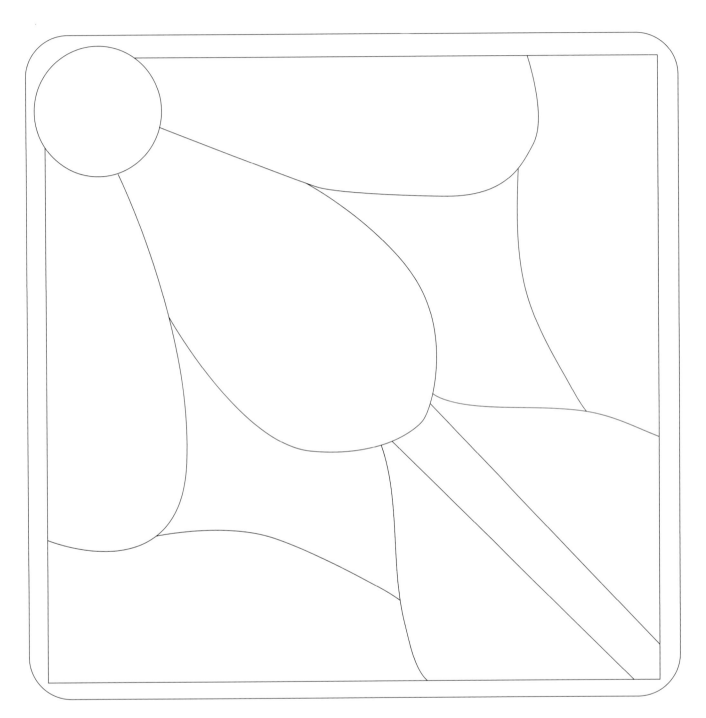

■ ▨ ■ enlarge the coneflower garden stone pattern to 111% ■ ▨ ■

lily and dragonfly
garden stone

A dragonfly sitting on a pink water lily makes a perfect subject for this garden stone. Brightly colored glass and shiny iridized dragonfly wings would look gorgeous submerged in a shallow pond. This stone is large enough to become the focal point of an entire garden design.

If you like, this water lily design can be traced on a wooden tabletop. Use the direct method to lay the tesserae on the tabletop, then protect the mosaic with a glass covering. Precut glass squares or tile squares would make a fabulous border.

MATERIALS AND TOOLS

- 18" (46cm) round stepping stone mold
- Glass: opaque cobalt, blue, opaque pink, iridized white, lime green, opaque turquoise and opaque orange
- Spray adhesive
- Adhesive paper
- Adhesive tape
- Pattern PAGE 121
- Scissors or mosaic shears
- Petroleum jelly
- Glass cutter

- Grozing pliers
- Running pliers
- Electric glass grinder
- Latex gloves
- Container
- Mixing tool
- Old towel and paint scraper
- Concrete
- Sealant

1 Cut pattern and glass

Make two copies of the pattern on page 121. Use one of the copies to cut out the glass pieces following the instructions on page 15.

2 Assemble mosaic

Assemble the cut-glass pieces inside the mold using the other copy of the pattern. Make sure that all the cut-glass pieces fit, and that there is at least a ⅛" (3mm) space between the tesserae.

3 Trim glass

If necessary, make adjustments to the cut-glass pieces using the electric glass grinder. Continue making adjustments until you're satisfied with the mosaic.

4 Finish mosaic

Prepare the mold with petroleum jelly. Using a light box or a sunny window and the other copy of the pattern, trace the pattern onto the back of the paper. Lay the pattern facedown in the mold. Trim an adhesive sheet to fit the pattern, then remove the backing from the sheet and lay it, sticky side up, on the pattern. Use tape to hold these pieces together. Lay the tesserae on the adhesive paper, using the pattern as a guide. Make sure there is at least ⅛" (3mm) between mosaic pieces. When complete, mix and pour concrete in the mold Use a hammer to settle the concrete in the mold.

5 Clean mosaic

When the mosaic is dry, carefully remove the mosaic from the mold. Clean the mosaic stone with an old towel and a scraper. Apply sealant when the concrete has completely set.

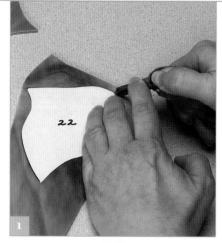

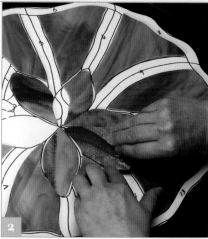

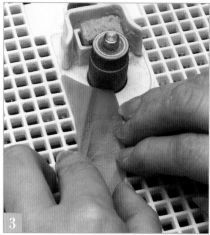

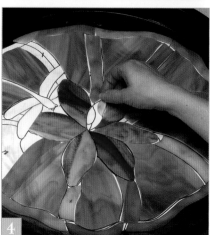

■ ■ ■ enlarge the lily and dragonfly garden stone pattern to 200%, then enlarge to 111% ■ ■ ■

Dragonfly Stepping Stone

The mosaic squares radiating out from the dragonfly give the impression of the frantic activity of this friendly insect.

White Flower Stepping Stone

Nuggets add dimension and iridized glass adds sparkle! What a fun way to remember a favorite flower.

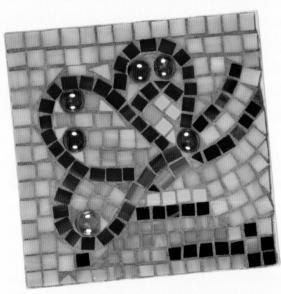

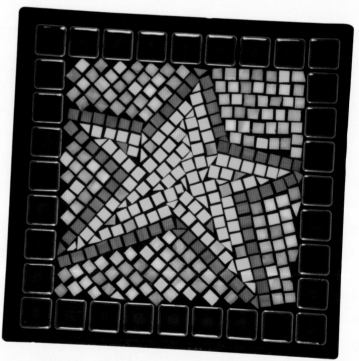

Child's Butterfly Tile

This tile uses the same fabric-inspired pattern as the Butterfly Tile project on page 54. Instead of broken glass, simple mosaic squares were used, making a project suitable for young crafters!

Star Stepping Stone

This star, while similar to the Catch a Falling Star project on page 58, uses mosaic squares for a very different effect. This project was a test of patience and symmetry, but the colors make it fun and the squares make it easy!

Field of Poppies

This large poppie window, based on the Summer Poppies project on page 106, is actually a stovetop backsplash! Made with beautifully colored and variegated glass, it provides a gorgeous backdrop that can easily be cleaned and looks terrific.

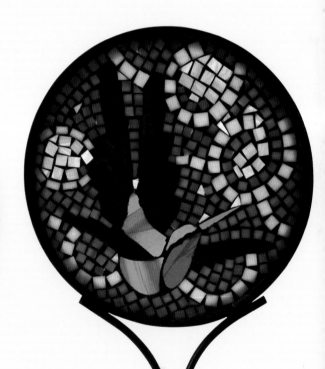

Fish In the Saucer

These birds are peering at a fish in their birdbath, or are they really admiring themselves? Either way, this is a fun way to add a bit of whimsy to your garden setting.

Hummingbird Garden Stake

This beautiful hummingbird flies with the speed of the wind, and causes turbulent conditions wherever he goes. Just look at that swirling grass! Garden stakes are a great way to bring the beauty of glass to your garden.

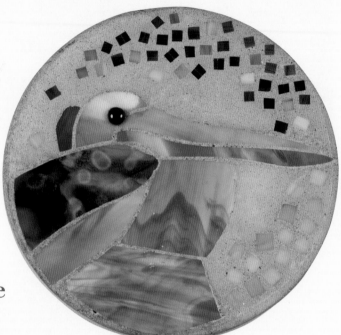

Sailboat Stepping Stone

This sailboat uses the same pattern as the Sailor's Delight project on page 74, but uses cut glass and nuggets as tesserae. Truly, a sailor's delight!

Seabird Stepping Stone

This southern bird perches on a wooden pier or railing in the Mississippi bayou. The texture of the glass and the use of a single glass nugget adds to the beauty of this project.

Glass Mosaic Photo

This is my favorite photo crafted as a mosaic! This project welcomes those who visit my home and brightens a corner all season long. The original photo was simplified, but the colors brought it to life.

Mosaic Tabletop

This beautiful masterpiece, created by Ken Williamson, is 6' (2m) across! Look closely to see the perched cardinals observing the bluebirds who are searching for their next snack. All the colors and textures make this tabletop unforgettable.

Mosaic Thermometer

Random pieces of glass and stone decorate this brick. Add a thermometer and this project becomes multi-purpose! There's room on the other side for a raincatcher or another mosaic.

Resources

Supplies

Tools and materials for mosaic projects are available at your local craft and hobby shops as well as at nurseries, garden centers, stained glass and home improvement stores. Look in your local phone book for stores near you.

Kaleidoscope Stained Glass
704 Main Street
Covington, KY 41011
(859) 491-2222
www.stainedglass4you.com
Glass, supplies, books, tools, restoration, custom designs and classes.

Organizations

The Society of American Mosaic Artists
P.O. Box 624
Ligonier, PA 15658
www.americanmosaics.org
Nonprofit organization dedicated to promoting mosaic art and artists.

Tile Heritage Foundation
P.O. Box 1850
Healdsburg, CA 95448
(707) 431-8453
www.tileheritage.org
Nonprofit organization dedicated to the appreciation and preservation of tile surfaces in America.

Art Glass Association
P.O. Box 2537
Zanesville, OH 43702
(866) 301-2421
www.artglassassociation.com
Association of glass artists, retailers, studios, suppliers and hobbyists that promotes awareness, knowledge and involvement for the growth of the art glass industry.

Stained Glass Association of America
10009 East 62nd Street
Raytown, MO 64133
(800) 438-7422
www.stainedglass.org
Nonprofit association dedicated to promoting the development and advancement of the stained and decorative art glass craft.

Index

A

abstract landscapes, 85, 95
adhesive paper, 12
adhesives, 10, 11
  cleaning residue, 16, 19
air bubbles, 19
assembling methods
  direct, 16
  indirect, 17

B

Birdbath Base, 46-49
Birdbath Saucer, 42-45
Blooming Daisies Garden Stone, 86-89
brass wire brush, 12
brick project, 62-65
Bunny Plaque, 102-105
butterflies, 38-41, 54-57, 125
Butterfly Feeder Stone, 38-41
Butterfly Tile, 54-57

C

Catch a Falling Star, 58-61
cathedral glass, 10
ceramic tiles, 24
children's projects, 51, 65
chimes, 50-53
china, 10, 14, 72
cleaning adhesive, 16, 19
clock, 70-73
color schemes, 31, 60, 73, 75
concrete, 10, 11, 39
  drying time, 41
  mixing, 40
Coneflower Garden Stone, 114-117
Country Clock, 70-73
cutting glass, 12, 15, 100

D

dragonflies, 121, 125

E

electric glass grinder, 12

F

Fish Fountain, 90-93
fixing problems, 19
Flower Box Posies, 26-29
flower patterns, 89, 101, 109, 117, 121
Flower Petal Ceiling Light, 34-37
flower pot project, 47-49
fountain, 90-93

G

Garden Chime, 50-53
garden stake, 123
garden stone projects, 86-89, 98-101, 110-113
Garden Tabletop, 82-85
Garden Thermometer, 66-69
glass, 10
  breaking, 14
  cutting technique, 15
  cutting tools, 12
  variations, 64
Glass Tile House Number, 30-33
glue; see also *adhesives*, 11
Goo Gone, 16
grid lines, 32
grout, 11, 18
  drying, 18
  extra, 44
  mixing with acrylic paint, 76

H

house number mosaic, 30-33

K

kitchen backsplash, 109, 123

L

Landscape Photo, 94-97
light shade project, 35-37
Lily and Dragonfly Garden Stone, 118-121
Liquid Nails Clear Adhesive, 11

M

marble, 10
materials; see also *tools*, 10, 11
memory stone, 39-41
mirror, 22-25
mirror glass, 10
molds, 12, 17

P

pattern transfer, 12, 19, 32
patterns
  birdbath, 45, 49
  blooming daisies, 89
  bunny plaque, 105
  butterfly tile, 57
  coneflower, 117
  fish fountain, 93
  flower box, 29
  garden brick, 65
  landscapes, 85, 97
  light shade, 37
  lily and dragonfly, 121
  poppies, 109
  sailors' delight, 77
  seaside village, 113
  stained glass flower, 81
  star, 61
  tabletop, 85
  thermometer, 69
  tulip stone, 101
photographs as patterns, 95, 96, 124
planters, 27-29, 47-49
pliers, 12
poppies, 109, 123
Preening Mirror, 22-25
problem solving, 19
putty knife, 12

R

rubber mallet, 14

S

sailboat, 74, 124
Sailor's Delight, 74-77
scissors, 12
sealants, 10, 11
  when to apply, 18, 53
Seaside Garden Brick, 62-65
Seaside Village Garden Stone, 110-113
shears, 12
Stained Glass Flower, 78-81
star mosaic, 61, 125
stepping stones, see *garden stones*
Summer Poppies, 106-109
surfaces, 10, 11

T

table tops, 82-85, 122
techniques, 14-19
terra cotta, 10
  pot project, 47-49
tesserae, 10, 14
  loose pieces, 19
thermometer, 66-69, 122
tile nippers, 12, 13
tiles, 10, 54-57, 69
tools, 12-13
tracing patterns, 12, 19
Tulips Garden Stone, 98-101

W

weathering, 10, 18, 28
Weldbond, 11
wind chimes, 50-53

North Light Books

EASY MOSAICS FOR YOUR HOME AND GARDEN
by Sarah Donnelly

These mosaics are surprisingly fun and easy to make! There's no messy grouting as you'll learn to use the stylish patterns and then simply mix, pour and embed. Simple, but so beautiful.

ISBN-13: 978-1-58180-129-7, pb, 128 pages, #31830
ISBN-10 1-58180-129-7

INSPIRED BY THE GARDEN
by Marie Browning

With 16 garden-inspired projects for both the inside and out, and using a range of crafting techniques and materials, this book showcases fun and sophisticated garden décor projects perfect for crafters of all skill levels.

ISBN-13: 978-1-58180-434-2, pb, 128 pages, #32630
ISBN-10 1-58180-434-2

HOME & GARDEN METALCRAFTS
by Jana Ewy

You'll find 15 functional and fun home and garden projects that make the most of the magical look of metal foil, wire and mesh, as well as a getting started section and so much more!

ISBN-13: 978-1-58180-330-3, pb, 96 pages, #32296
ISBN-10: 1-58180-330-3

These books and other fine North Light titles are available from your local art & craft retailer or bookstore or online suppliers.